Ernst von Elterlein

Beethoven's Pianoforte Sonatas

Ernst von Elterlein

Beethoven's Pianoforte Sonatas

ISBN/EAN: 9783742881656

Manufactured in Europe, USA, Canada, Australia, Japa

Cover: Foto ©Thomas Meinert / pixelio.de

Manufactured and distributed by brebook publishing software
(www.brebook.com)

Ernst von Elterlein

Beethoven's Pianoforte Sonatas

Beethoven's

Pianoforte Sonatas

EXPLAINED FOR THE LOVERS OF THE MUSICAL ART

BY

ERNST VON ELTERLEIN

TRANSLATED FROM THE GERMAN BY

EMILY HILL

With a Preface by E. Pauer

SECOND EDITION.

LONDON

W. REEVES, 185, FLEET STREET, E.C.

(Office of the "Musical Standard.")

1879.

PREFACE.

THE transcendent beauty and the exceeding importance of Beethoven's Pianoforte Sonatas are facts now universally recognized. It is a healthy sign of musical progress and an undeniable proof of the spread of an improved taste and of a genuine appreciation of the excellent, in musical art, that various nations now emulate each other's efforts in issuing correct and excellent editions of these great works. We now possess good and correct editions of Beethoven's Sonatas at such cheap and modest prices, that the entire collection of the thirty-eight Sonatas is to be had for the same price which our grandfathers paid for a single one; and this remarkable reduction of price has undoubtedly contributed in no small degree to the universal popularity which this unrivalled monument of musical art has now everywhere obtained.

To describe the contents of a musical work is always a difficult task; and it cannot be denied that a great deal of nonsense has been written, in the endeavour to analyze, describe, and annotate the works of great musical composers. No author has had to suffer more from the indiscreet zeal of busy shallow annotators than Ludwig van Beethoven; no other composer's works have been so unwarrantably and unnecessarily overladen with weak description. The small work, *Beethoven's Clavier-Sonaten für Freunde der Tonkunst erläutert von Ernst von Elterlein*, stands forth as an honourable exception amidst the host of insipid commentaries on the great master's works—the multitudinous explanations that explain nothing. Elterlein's book appeared in Leipsic, in 1856. It has, since that year, gone through many editions, and has obtained great and deserved popularity in Germany. Although Herr von Elterlein is a musical amateur, he writes with the ripe knowledge and thorough understanding of a practical musician; and as the merits of his book speak for themselves, any further praise would be superfluous.

Herr von Elterlein's design is not so much to describe the beauties of Beethoven's Sonatas, as to direct the performer's attention to these beauties, and to point out the leading and characteristic features of each separate piece. It was reserved for Beethoven to give expression, in his Sonatas, to the highest and loftiest feelings of the human heart. In these unapproachable master-pieces, he is not only pathetic, but also sincere, humorous, tender, graceful, simple —in short, he expresses in them every varying shade of feeling that can agitate the human heart. To point out all these varying shades, to indicate to the earnest student of Beethoven all these numberless beauties, is the object of Herr von Elterlein's book; and every musical student or amateur can safely trust him as a competent and agreeable guide.

An English translation of this valuable little work is, therefore, most opportune; it will, undoubtedly, assist many a lover of Beethoven's music to appreciate more keenly the beauties of the great master's Sonatas, and will, if possible, enhance his admiration of what may truly be called a book of wisdom.

London, June, 1875.   E. PAUER.

CONTENTS.

—⊸❃⊶—

First Part.

THE SONATA IN GENERAL.

THE Sonata is the greatest and most original production in the province of pianoforte music—its highest exercise and its loftiest aim. Beauty, the ideal of all artistic efforts, may be found in the simplest music, but perfection requires the highest form.

The Sonata may be considered the most perfect form of pianoforte music. The theoretical reasons for this statement are most successfully propounded by Marx, in the third part of his "Compositionslehre." Marx there explains the development of the different forms of pianoforte music in organic order. He begins with the study, proceeds to the fantasia, variation, and rondo, and then to the Sonata, the key-stone and crowning point of all the forms. In another way, Krüger, in his "Beitragen für Leben und Wissenschaft der Tonkunst," arrives at the same result. Like Marx, he establishes a system of musical forms, of which he makes the song form the centre : first, the forms that preceded the song form, preludes, toccatas, fantasias; secondly, the song form, variations, rondos, fugues ; thirdly, that which followed the song form, the union of existing song forms, the Sonata and the Symphony. Krüger considered the three primary forms to be the prelude, song, and Sonata, and that out of these all the others have been developed. The great importance of the Sonata form generally—a form which is also the foundation of the symphony, string quartett, &c. —especially shows itself in its capability of forming a higher union of the other forms, namely, the song, variation, rondo, and fugue. This was, in fact, indicated by Krüger in the expression, " composition of existing song forms." Indeed, in the Sonata all these forms return, and are, so to speak, fused into a concrete and actual unity. According to this view, the Sonata is the organic product of these forms, and this the Beethoven Sonata pre-eminently proves.

If we consider more closely the construction of the Sonata, we shall find it to be divided into several movements—two, three, four, five, or even more—and the plurality of movements may be generally stated as the formal principle of the composition. The particular character, however, of the life-picture which a work depicts must always be considered its determining basis. " The soul moulds its own body." (" Die Seele schafft sich ihren Leib.") Musicians must, therefore, in this respect, desist from laying down binding laws and unchangeable principles. Köstlin (in Vischer's " Aesthetik.") and Marx (in " Beethoven's Leben and Schaffen ") have, in a searching and ingenious manner, propounded and undertaken to prove that the three or four-movement form is the normal principle of construction. Indeed, most Sonatas do contain three or four movements. But, on the other hand, it may be urged that, as will presently be shown, in many of Beethoven's Sonatas, even in some of his most important ones, the two-movement principle decidedly predominates, and to this from the three and four-movement form the great master of the Sonata, in the last of these works, (Op. III.), significantly returns. Marx says, in another place, " That the ideas here set forth are not binding definitions, (who can bind the mind ?) ; but only expositions of the principles that may lie at the origin of the form, it being certainly quite clear that the three is as practicable as the four-part form, and that in the future the two and the several movement form will be equally justifiable." This freedom of form appears also in the design and arrangement of the different movements. It will be decided by the character of the entire work, whether, for example, the so-called *andante* or *adagio*, generally the slow movement, forms the second or third movement, (in the four-movement form), or whether it should stand at the commencement. It is surely unnecessary to say, that the point in discussion is not the want of form in the composition, but the model on which that form has been framed. It must be steadfastly maintained that the idea is the only decisive principle of the form. This brings us from the form to the matter of the Sonata.

The actual essence of music may be described as the "far dark currents of the soul, the fleeting life, the constant whirl of the world into which all existence and all repose are drawn; as all that rises, hovers, and trembles in the air, and in the heart of man, all that the soul re-echoes to itself from the varied phenomena of movement." *(Krüger.)* Or we may say, with Carriere (Aesthetik), "It is music which discovers and explains for us the beautiful in the world and in the mind, or still more which shows us, in the movements of the world and the mind, that inner life which a spiritual nature reveals, so that, amid the external action in which we are engaged, the conditions of mind and soul may express themselves, or through sound make us acquainted with the things of their life. The representation of the ideal in a concrete form is the aim of music as it is of art. The tone-art shows the course of the different feelings—is a clear copy of the real personal progress of existence and of its life melodies." As this holds good of music in general, the substance of the Sonata may be briefly described as the subjective life of mind and soul. As Köstlin says, the object of the Sonata is to display a rich, expressive, and subjective state of feeling, whether this spreads itself broadly out as a fine, characteristic, multifarious train of emotional images, or whether it shows, in the form of a great tone-picture, one of the different phases of the uniform sentiment which runs through the emotional life.

What instrument could better adapt itself to the representation of this than the pianoforte? The pianoforte, says Köstlin, since it blends harmony with melody, and yet gives the former into the hands of the subject, is the principle organ for the free, full, and safe custody of the latter; in this instrument the subject is introduced purely for its own sake, and is thus in a position to express itself clearly and entirely. The piano is an orchestra in miniature. Marx calls it the ideal instrument.

It is well knows that Hanslick has again recently brought forward his charge of the emptiness of music. He considers it to be only "sounding forms," and compares music with arabesque; but Brendel (Neue Zeitschrift für musik, vol. 42, No. 8) and Carriere (Aesthetik, vol. 2, page 322) have thoroughly refuted this opinion. Vischer also, (Aesthetik, Part 3, page 790) shows the contradiction in which Hanslick involves himself, when he is afterwards obliged to admit that "thought and feeling, the dearest and most powerful impulses of the human mind," are the "substance" of music. But Brendel aptly says, "the feelings of the soul are the substance of music —material which is equally available for all artists. Now this does not represent mind as having only a vague external connection with technical principles, as a something fleeting and vanishing. Mind and substance are indispensable to music; the succession of sounds is the direct expression of them, the thing itself, and not mere form. Nevertheless, the whole life of music rests on a real phsycological basis, and we have no mere combinations of sound to deal with."

Let us now turn to the historical realities of the art. Before occupying ourselves exclusively with Beethoven, it is necessary, for many reasons, to give a brief historical account of the Sonata, from its commencement to its perfection by Beethoven. For the ground-work of this sketch, as far as the time of Haydn, we will make use of the excellent contributions to the history of the Sonata, by J. Faisst, in *The Cäcilia*, a newspaper now discontinued.

Second Part.

THE SONATA BEFORE BEETHOVEN.

THE earliest beginnings of the Sonata are found towards the close of the seventeenth century. The first Sonatas appeared in 1681, for violin solo, by Henry Biber; then, in 1683, there appeared twelve Sonatas for violin, violoncello, and piano, by the violinist, Corelli. But more important as a composer of pianoforte Sonatas was Johann Kuhnau, Sebastian Bach's predecessor. He first wrote a Sonata in " B " in " Neuer Clavierübung anderer Theil." Generally speaking, the form is the present one, the Sonata consisting of a quick, a slow, and then a quick movement. The style of writing is polyphonic, but the work fails in inward æsthetic connection. Kuhnau's next work appeared, in 1696, under the title of "Fresh Fruit for the Piano; or, Seven Sonatas for the Pianoforte, excellent in design and style, by Johann Kuhnau." These Sonatas show progress in form and in matter; they are full of energy, vivacity, fresh grace, and also of deep feeling. They consist entirely of four or five movements, and the contrast of the quiet and agitated movement is found in many cases. The polyphonic treatment is predominant, though the homophonic sometimes breaks through, launching forth into free melodies. Single movements show yet greater artistic merit. Kuhnau is intellectually associated with Handel, by free polyphony and an energetic or clear treatment of melody. An inward æsthetic connection is already discernible in single movements. The next composer to be mentioned in this department is Mattheson. A Sonata appeared by him, in 1713, "dedicated to whoever will play it best." It consists of one movement only; the treatment generally is richer than with former composers, nor is the theme without merit; but the working of the materials shows more external brilliancy than internal wealth.

We come to Domenico Scarlatti. In the first decade of the eighteenth century, he wrote "30 Sonate per il clavicembalo," and "6 Sonate per il cembalo." Every Sonata contains two parts, the present so-called fantasia (durchführungstheil) part, and the third part being blended into one. A similarity to the two-part song-form prevails. The two-part form predominates; the style of writing is more fitted to the instrument than was that of Scarlatti's predecessors; and the crossing of the hands claims notice. With respect to the matter

of the Sonatas, Scarlatti himself describes them as
"clever tricks of art." They are bright, fresh,
lively and intelligent, and often overflow with
humour, with touches also of a softer and more
earnest feeling; though of deeper intentions there
is no trace.

Scarlatti did not give a new form to the Sonata,
in the sense of making a new combination of existing movements, but he produced, in a style of writing
freed from the fetters of polyphony and fitted to the
true nature of the instrument, a form regularly
matured from the early kernel of the single-move-
ment Sonata. This form, as the standard, if
not for all, at least for the most important movement
of the Sonata, as the most considerable generally
among the non-polyphonic forms of an instrumental
movement, must have first developed a degree of
excellence corresponding to the lofty aim of the
Sonata, before what afterwards happened could have
been possible, namely, the giving to the Sonata,
as a combination of several movements, a regular
and reasonable shape.

Francesco Durante, the Italian, must not be
omitted; he produced one publication: "Sonate per
cembalo divise in studiei divertimenti." In formal
construction, these Sonatas are a transition between
the song-form and the Sonata-form; they are homo-
phonically written. Looked at with respect to
historical development, they are deeper than Scarlatti's Sonatas; in a free, natural style of writing,

they are a stage beyond Kuhnau; while, as regards matter, they may be called valuable and intelligent.

We now approach that musical giant, Sebastian Bach, of whom we will specify two Sonatas, the C minor and D minor. The Sonata form—the combination of several movements into one whole—reappears with him. In the Sonatas mentioned, he certainly is not, either in form or style, equal in freedom to Scarlatti; he stands nearer to Kuhnau; but he is far superior to the latter in richness and a free command of means; and, on the other hand, he shows himself in advance of Scarlatti, in that he combined several movements into a whole, in accordance with the characteristic style of the Sonata, so that a highly intellectual inner meaning was more apparent than before. Altogether, Bach is the intervening transition step.

The twelve Sonatas by Father Martini, " per l'organo vel cembalo," are another intermediary work. Judging by the character of their composition, the Sonatas should have been styled "for the piano" —not "for the organ." In form, they are a medium between the so-called suite and the Sonata proper, being a mixture of polyphony and homophony, with skilful workmanship, and plenty of intelligence and life.

From the middle of the eighteenth century till the death of Emanuel Bach, in 1788, when the Sonata acquired a regular form, and one adequate to its conception, was the beginning of a new period. Pianoforte literature increased rapidly. Faisst reckons in all 208 Sonatas and 35 composers. After the true, or at least the principal form, had been found for the single movement of the Sonata, the object was to give to the Sonata, as a whole formed of several movements, a systematic shape corresponding to its design. These Sonatas, therefore, regularly contain several movements. But this union of several movements into one whole took place in many different ways, and is not so much to be considered as an expression of greater freedom as of indecision, of a striving after a suitable form. The three-movement form predominates, two and four movements are the exception; in the latter, the minuett already appears as the second movement. The form of the single movement is still partly like Scarlatti's, partly more perfect than his was. Movements with a second theme already appear, but the latter is more like a complement to the first theme than a contrast to it; its substance is not so characteristically different, its existence is often doubtful; hence the weakness of this period. We observe further an enrichment and extension of the song-form, although only an outward one, for its internal expansion leads it into the rondo and Sonata-form. Movements with variations, in the dance-forms, the minuett, and polonaise, and more rarely the rondo-form, already appear. The most important name in this period is that of Emanuel

Bach, while Johann Christian Bach and Leopold Mozart are also briefly to be mentioned.

The Sonatas of Johann Christian Bach are full of fire, humour, and fresh grace ; his style of writing is like that of Haydn and Mozart. In Leopold Mozart's Sonatas we seem to be already listening to his great son, so much do their style and spirit remind us of the latter.

Emanuel Bach's works bear witness especially to a refined, intelligent, exceedingly intellectual and pleasing nature ; we feel with him that everything is the expression of the heart, and that all is fresh-ness, strength and noble feeling. He is Haydn's forerunner both in the form and matter of his works. The complete and perfect three-movement form becomes a regular principle of construction with him. His Sonatas contain, generally, a first move-ment, *allegro*, in the short Sonata-form ; a second movement, *andante*, in the song-form ; and a third movement, *presto*, in the rondo-form. His style of writing is mostly homophonic. Brendel says of him, in his excellent " History of Music," " Bach, by representing, contrary to former composers, the individual mind and feeling of the writer, directly brought in the new instrumental music, and by setting forth individuality in its changing and diverse forms, became the founder of modern music." His chief works are his " Sonatas for Connoisseurs and Amateurs."

A new epoch now began : the grandest which

the Sonata has ever known, that of Haydn, Mozart, and Beethoven. As in the principal kinds of instrumental music, Haydn appears as an epoch-maker, a genius breaking through the old boundaries —in proof of which we have only to refer to his symphonies and quartetts—so also the simple piano-forte Sonata received from him an important im-petus and development, both in form and manner. Although the three-movement form must be spoken of as Emanuel Bach's work, the contributions made by Haydn to the progress of the Sonata were: that he repeated the principal theme of the first part of a movement in the third part, that he regularly settled the second, so-called fantasia part, and the third, so-called repetition part, into the Sonata form; that he reduced what had before been the mere humour and caprice of the composer, and in many of the earlier works had not even been found at all, into an un-changing principle of construction; that by these means he raised, enriched and amplified the single movement—which means the Sonata generally—that he reached a higher unity, and created a firmer and more uniform whole. Progress in the matter of the Sonata was now within narrow limits. The chief thought had to gain importance by repetition; more especially as Haydn had given to it a decided and characteristic expression, which he firmly maintained throughout the move-ment. Indeed, the principal movements of the Haydn Sonata have a uniform fundamental thought stamped on them. Not only does the single movement show this unity, but the collective movements of the Sonata form a much more uniform whole, follow more from a determined basis, and are much more closely connected together than in the works of previous writers. I say "much more," for the unity that we find in Beethoven, a unity that was close and despotic, because it rested on a psychological basis, is not yet to be found; we have rather, if I may use the expression, the stringing together of several movements united by one common sentiment. But what is the ruling sentiment? It is that spirit of näive and child-like cheerfulness, that teasing play of jest and mirth, that roguish humour, that caprice and frolicksomeness; in short, all the thoughts and feelings of Haydn's whole artistic nature run through all his instrumental music. Köstlin well says that Haydn brought in the epoch of free style, the golden age and spring-time of the musical art, that with him music becomes conscious that she is not a mere system and science, but a free impulse and a lyric poem. Brendel calls Haydn the greatest master of jest and humour. However limited Haydn's world may be, compared to the boundless vistas which Beethoven has revealed to us, however little Haydn's child-like nature may show us of the deep secrets of the soul, yet he is in his own sphere so original, so brimming over with *Genialität*, that a place belongs to him among the first of the tone-artists; and he who

has thoroughly entered into the gigantic conceptions
of Beethoven may still turn back, now and then, to a
Sonata of " Father Haydn," to enjoy, as it were, a
picture of his own past childhood, and to pass once
again through the first paradise of life. Among
Haydn's many Sonatas, two only need here be
referred to as prominent works, the one in E flat
major, and a smaller one in B minor.

Mozart was Haydn's real successor in the department of the Sonata. He gave it a further development in many respects. Mozart adhered also to the
principle received from Haydn, of starting with a
definite and expressive theme, and making it the
basis of the movement. But this did not satisfy him ;
he wanted a something by which a greater diversity,
together with a more intellectual unity, should be
attained, and this something was the *cantabile*,
or the second subject which Mozart introduced
into the first movement of the Sonata. On
the whole he composed longer and richer phrases
of melody, larger and broader periods, established
a more defined difference between light and shade,
divided both into larger divisions of time, and
precise periods, and thus produced a definite
distinction between the tender and the vigorous
parts, a greater clearness and decision in the
form and in the sequence of thought. Another
characteristic feature of his Sonatas, is the utmost
beauty of form, which, in system, symmetry and
regularity, shows itself alike in small and great.

This is the natural result of a perfect and harmonious nature. As Brendel and others have strikingly shown, Mozart's artistic individuality revealed, both in public and private, the purest harmony of mind and soul, a quiet self-contained balance of powers; a condition of the inner life in which the moral struggles are hushed, or at most form but the far dark back-ground. This primary adjustment imparted that gracefulness of mind, which is yet another characteristic feature of his music. This is such an essential quality with him, that when he depicts violent passion, he holds himself far aloof from roughness; everything is so closely wrapt in a pleasant dress, that the passion is, so to speak, stifled. It is only Mozart, the artist, who struggles; Mozart, the man, came out conqueror long ago. In this respect, Mozart's symphony and quintett in G minor are especially characteristic. As regards the Sonatas, it must be acknowledged at once that Mozart stands far higher in other departments of instrumental music. The most important Sonata is unquestionably the C minor with the fantasia before it; beside this rank the F major, A minor, the Sonata for two performers in F major, and a few others. On the foundation laid by the Haydn and Mozart Sonata, Beethoven reared his gigantic edifice, to the consideration of which we now turn.*

---

* From this historical sketch Clementi may with propriety be omitted, for his *forte* was the *technique* of pianoforte playing, in which Beethoven even scarcely excelled him.

Third Part.

BEETHOVEN.

AS Beethoven, in his instrumental music generally, took his starting point from Haydn and Mozart, so in his Sonatas he first trod in the footsteps of these composers. But when he had reached greater maturity and independence, Beethoven left these paths, struck out a new way and took a fresh aim, raised both the form and matter of the Sonata, breathed into it a spirit, such as Haydn and Mozart had never known; in a word, gave to it that peculiar, and as yet unreached, depth and grandeur, which ever and anon awaken the unqualified admiration of the true lover of music. Unlike Haydn and Mozart, Beethoven was so entirely absorbed in this kind of music, and displayed in it so much of the essential character of his genius, that Hand, in his " Aesthetik der Tonkunst," comes to the conclusion that Beethoven's originality is pre-eminently recognizable in his

Sonatas. This is asserting too much, for the strong point of his music rests really in the symphonies and quartetts, though it is true that the Sonata gives us one of our clearest conceptions of this com-poser. The stages of Beethoven's artistic growth may doubtless be traced with the greatest certainty in his Sonatas; for even Beethoven was not all at once what he became in his prime. The gradual growth and ripening of his intellect—surely one of the most interesting psychological periods in the course of a great artist's development—is more clearly illustrated by his Sonatas than by his other works. Nowhere else are those fine, gradual changes, that progress towards an ever increasing independ-ence, so noticeable and so traceable. On the other hand, what an unbridged chasm exists between the second and third symphonies, between the quartetts, op. 18, and those three constellations, op. 59. The Sonatas, surrounding and uniting these works, form the intermediary stages, build the bridge over the chasm, and solve the problem. If the question be now asked, What are the contents of the Beethoven Sonatas? it can only be fully answered by the following explanation of the different works. Mean-while we must set forth some general points of view, and the common ground from which the consideration of particular parts arises; in other words, the nature of Beethoven's artistic indivi-duality, and of his instrumental music generally, must be shown in its universal features, in order to get the surest foundation for the perception of the particulars and specialities.

The characteristic of his genius is, in my opinion, a rare, rich fancy, closely allied with a dreamy, unfathomable depth of soul,* irradiated by a lofty intellectual consciousness, and sustained by a strong will and a decisive character.† In Beethoven, fancy, feeling, intellect, and character are developed with equal power and significance, and in strict harmony with each other. These, it seems to me, are the foundation of the finest passages; nor can this close connection of fancy, feeling, intellect and character be preserved except by a strong subjectiveness, not one-sided or wrapt-up in itself, but in unison with objective qualities equally potent.

In contrast to Mozart and other composers, Beethoven has been called a pre-eminently subjective artist, with whom form was subservient to subjective matter. There is some truth in this statement, but it must be taken *cum grano salis*, for, with all his self-absorption, Beethoven had more true objectiveness than many of the *soi-disant* objective composers. It is inconceivable that such fully developed tensely

---

* Kullak says, in his excellent work on the Beautiful in Music: " No one has ever felt more devoutly than Bach, more happily than Mozart, or with more gigantic power than Beethoven."

† Richard Wagner says, (" Kunstwerk der Zukunft ") with regard to the C minor symphony, " Beethoven raised the expression of his music almost to a moral determination."

strung subjectiveness could exist without a struggle, at least not without deep stirring excitement could it have come into being, and in contact with other existences. Do we not find it especially so with Beethoven? Köstlin says, that with Beethoven music, being a reflection of himself and his connection with the objective world, is alike the attraction and repulsion of the subjective through the objective into the innermost and all pervading *ego*. All these pecularities appear prominently in Beethoven's instrumental music; and it has long been recognized that his *forte* lies in this, and not in vocal music.

Concerning the peculiarities of Beethoven's instrumental music, Brendel, with admirable conciseness, thus writes, in his " Musical History :" " The chief characteristic of Beethoven's instrumental music is the increased power of the subject-matter resulting in the heightening and extending of all the means of expression. Following this increased significance of the matter, we see a striving after the utmost clearness of expression, by which music alone, not united to words, may represent definite states of mind. In earlier times, with Haydn and Mozart, the common character of instrumental music was a free play of vague, general expression. Beethoven, on the contrary, expressed definite situations, and pourtrayed clearly recognizable states of mind. Closely allied with this was his endeavour to set a poetical image before the mind of the hearer, while the dramatic life of his compositions was evolved by development of the matter. Mozart's aim had been an intelligent and logical working out of the form which a piece of music took. But with· Beethoven this was no longer a guiding principle, and the tone-poet follows his poetical object by bringing before us a soul-picture, rich in various moods and feelings. The humorous element also plays its parts in his works."

Beethoven's Sonatas, as the reflection of the general artistic personality of their composer, are conspicuous for increased dimensions, for the representation of definite frames of mind, and for their poetic tendency. Certainly the range is in no way so comprehensive as, for example, it is in the symphony. In the latter the sentiment is preponderatingly objective and general, though in the light of a Beethoven subjectiveness. In the Sonatas Beethoven refers only to his innermost self. Buried in the secrets of his own heart, to the piano alone does he confide the concerns of his inmost soul. Before examining these works, we must say a few words on the style and periods of Beethoven's creations. It has been already intimated that at first Beethoven trod in the paths of his predecessors, Haydn and Mozart, yet in the works belonging to that time his individuality continually becomes more conspicuous. This is the first period. Now, Beethoven has emancipated himself, stands alone, has reached maturity and independence, has become a man, in the fullest sense of the word. This is the second period. In the course of his artistic life, partly in consequence of outward, partly of inward circumstances, Beethoven continually retreats into himself; he, so to speak, isolates his soul's life, raises his subjectiveness to a point at which the artist appears an isolated being, and only the most individual feelings are represented. This is called the third period. To the first period the first twenty or thirty works are generally assigned; to the second, those up to a hundred; and to the third period, the works beyond that number. To draw a definite boundary line is in the nature of things impossible; since then, as now, the numbers prefixed to the works did not, in a great measure, at all correspond to the time of their composition; therefore, the so-called opus numbers can afford no criterion. Then, again, everything in Beethoven's works flows in such a living stream that abstract divisions cannot be set up in single works; the transitions are too fine. Marx, in his excellent book on Beethoven, goes too far when he ignores these periods. In its profoundest depths, Beethoven's style certainly is but one; that *something* which distinguishes him from other masters does not appear for the first time in his later works. Yet such characteristic differences appear in this unity, that each period surely has its *raison d'être.*

Fourth Part.

BEETHOVEN'S SONATAS.

BEETHOVEN'S Sonatas may be divided into several groups; but, deferring this for the present, we will, without further preface, closely examine the separate works, according to their opus numbers, and reserve the other consideration of them for the last part.

OP. 2, No. 1, F MINOR.

Appeared in 1796. Dedicated to Joseph Haydn.

This Sonata is distinguished throughout by the consistent development of a fundamental thought, by which, with much diversity of detail, a uniform character is given to the whole, or, as Marx puts it, a series of moods and feelings are psychologically developed as a subjective whole.

A certain discontentedness runs through the first movement, *allegro*, F minor, $\frac{2}{4}$ time; a mild restlessness of mind, a half shy seeking for something and

not finding it; to see which we need only look at
the characteristic form of the two chief subjects, and
at the opposite working of them (compare Marx,
" Beethoven," vol. 1, p. 122). What then remains
but quietly to submit? Does not the third subject,
shortly before the end of the first part, and also
before the end of the whole movement, the passage marked *con express*, express this? There is all
through the movement a breath of really passionate
yearning, but only a breath; it does not come to
a real struggle, and to sharp contrasts; the piece
has a sort of mild sharpness about it. The second
movement, *adagio*, F major, ¾ time, Marx calls a
child's prayer. " It comforts if it does not find a
hearing, yet the anxiety depicted in the first movement has not disappeared, but in the tributary
subject quietly and unobtrusively makes itself felt."
A true contentment of mind speaks through these
strains; it is only in passing that anything painful
arises to darken the picture; but the cloudlet soon
disappears, and it is clear sunshine again. Few of
Beethoven's movements bear so prominently this
stamp of mildness. This gentleness is also partly
expressed in the other movements. The repose of
the *adagio* was but passing. In the third movement,
menuetto allegretto, F minor, ¾ time, the mind of the
tone-poet falls back into the discontent and restless
yearning of the first movement. " No rest and no
peace " (keine Rast und keine Ruh) is the impression
produced by the Minuet and by the Trio in F major,

and the climax of this sentiment in the second part
of the minuet is very fine. But now, in the fourth
movement, *prestissimo*, F minor, ¢ time, a storm
rises in the soul; as Marx finely says, when fortune
fails we behold the courage of pain, the wrath of
a noble mind, struggling with unworthy troubles,
and, if not crowned with conquest, worthy of victory.
In this movement, the fundamental idea of the whole
rises to real passion, which is excellently expressed
by the sweeping trills and the well-marked chief
theme. Only for a moment, in the first part, is
a quieter sentiment perceptible, then, at the beginning of the second part, a soothing melody predominates for a time, and the expression becomes
deeply fervent. But this picture of bliss gradually
disappears, for the waves of passion sweep onward
again, ever stronger and more irrepressible, the
storm and rushing begin afresh and victoriously
keep the field till the end of the whole. The *finale*
is indisputably the finest movement of the Sonata;
it is beautifully rounded, and the distribution of
light and shade excellent. Lenz, in "Beethoven
et ses Trois Styles," says of it: "Un morceau si
franc, si dramatique, qu'il n'en existait pas dans le
temps qui pût lui être comparé." The radical
principle of the Sonata is decidedly Mozartish,
whether we consider the form or the matter,
especially the principal subject, though there is
no doubt that in the *finale*, both in the general
and in detail, the later Beethoven already shows

himself: the elevation and energy of the last movement, and the transition from the second to the
third part are true signs of Beethoven.

OP. 2, No. 2, A MAJOR.

Appeared in 1796.   *Dedicated to Joseph Haydn.*

This Sonata is distinguished by an almost equally
uniform and consistent, though not quite so close
and clear a development of the primary thought as
the preceding work, which, while partly surpassing
in originality, it is throughout inferior to in elevation
of style.   In the first movement, *allegro vivace*, $\frac{2}{4}$
time, Beethoven instantly struck quite a new chord.
How courageously and self-reliantly the first theme is
announced, how boldly and briskly it is carried out,
how striking are the scales and modulations which
we hear!   A youthful and even wanton humour is
the leading thought.   Marx sees, in fancy, a restless boy, who does not know where to let off his
overflowing fulness of life.   Notwithstanding, a
deep, yearning feeling rises up, just as if this wanton
play of humour could not possibly ensure true and
lasting satisfaction.   This is the tributary subject
in C minor, which appears in A minor in the second
part.   The whole movement is cast in one mould, and
is full of a fresh and uniformly harmonious expression
of feeling.   Here, already, the original genius of Beethoven decidedly appears, the first dawnings of the
later Beethoven humour are perceptible.   The move-

ment contains passages, such as the one which, at the entrance of the second part, is first worked up in C, and then comes to rest in the same key, in the passage further on in E major, just before the return of the first subject, and others also, whose origin would be sought for in vain in Mozart's principles. In the second movement, *largo appassionato*, D major, ⁴ time, feeling, humour, and fancy gather themselves together and give place to a more exalted tone. There is something sublime in the development of those quiet, measured strains of melodies and harmonies. Lenz remarks that the piece reminds one of Handel's style. Profound but subdued agitation pervades the movement. Very impressive is the entrance of the D minor in the second half of the piece, the diversion into B major, and then the return into D with the repetition of the first subject in a higher octave ; by this, and by the conclusion which of necessity follows, a quiet touch of glory is added to the picture, and the whole is rounded off in beauty. Marx well says : "the song is quiet and solemn, like the thoughts of a noble mind alone under the starry firmament ;" and the entrance of the minor, he says, produces a thrilling emotion, as if words like death and eternity had fallen on the heart. The *scherzo allegretto* A major, ⁴ time, which follows as the third movement, is a lively bright composition, "charmingly alluring," recalling, as does also the minor (trio), the Haydn-Mozart minuett form, and in no way attaining to the originality

of the first two movements.   Lenz finds in the trio
the character of the Russian and Sclavonic melodies
generally.   The fourth movement, *rondo grazioso*,
A major, ⁴ time, is a picture of easy, cheerful
existence; there is no trace of the Beethoven
humour, such as we found in the first movement;
this movement, the chief theme especially, is decidedly Mozartishly conceived; there is an agreeable
play of sounds, but a deeper meaning is wanting.
The formal musical structure is, however, interesting, the rondo-form being originally treated.   On
this point I would refer the reader to the third
part of Marx's " Compositionslehre," in which
he speaks of the movement as the model for, and
highest realization of, the rondo-form.   The Sonata,
as a whole, consists of two not quite equally
good parts; the two last movements do not fully
correspond throughout, in style and expression, to
the two first.   Marx also thinks that the psychological unity of the last movements is not in accordance with the first movements.

OP. 2, No. 3, C MAJOR.

Appeared in 1796.   Dedicated to Joseph Haydn.

This Sonata also, though resting as a whole on
Mozart's principles, reveals the later Beethoven in
particular passages, and, with the exception, perhaps,
of the second movement, it has a steadily developed
uniform idea lying at its basis.   A bright, active life,

shows itself in the first movement, *allegro con brio*, C major, ⁴₄ time ; a youthful freshness and vigour run through it. Nor is gracefulness wanting, as the passages marked *dolce*, in G major, and C major, respectively, in the first and second parts abundantly prove. On the other hand, the picture is not without its humorous side (motive at bar 19, before the conclusion of the first part). Storm and hurry are well depicted by the rolling up and down of the octaves. The so-called fantasia part contains some excellent passages, and moves more freely than in the works of earlier composers, but the most original part seems to me to be the *point d'orgue* on the chord of A flat major, followed by an interesting cadence, leading back to the first theme, and bringing in a magnificent and powerful conclusion. In the whole of the Coda, Beethoven boldly discards the strict sonata-form, for the free form of the fantasia. A deep devoutness pervades the first theme of the second movement, *adagio*, E major, ²₄ time, a feeling of inward contentment and happiness breathes through its tones. Soon, however, with the appearance of the E minor, a yearning impulse, not without pain and sorrow, is manifested. (Entrance of the A and B minor in *fortissimo*). Further on, the first theme comes soothingly in again, and in C major *fortissimo* it even becomes the expression of courageous confidence. It is true that the yearning begins again, but it is materially subdued, the pain is dulled, and the first theme is heard for the last time, an octave higher—sounding as it were from a glorified height—and, in a quiet, beatified mood, the movement ends. The colouring, the shading, the modulations, everything is fresh, new, original, sometimes even magical; it is certainly tone-poetry, soul-painting, such as was peculiar to Beethoven alone. After this movement what can the third movement—the *allegro scherzo*, C major, ⅜ time —mean? Its character is careless, self-satisfied cheerfulness; the form is still that of the Haydn-Mozart minuett, the Beethoven scherzo has not yet appeared. The trio in A minor is not without originality, with its almost wilful sequence of the upper and lower octaves; the former, restless, fleeting, surging, in contrast to the hopefulness of the latter. The tone-colouring of the whole is original, and an excellent preparation for the character of the *finale*. This fourth movement, *allegro assai*, C major, ⅜ time, is full of the most sparkling life, a little Bacchanalia, the product of bold, youthful petulance, a piece of a period of storm and rushing. The motive, in F major (*dolce*), in the middle of the movement, forms an agreeable contrast, and so much the more increases the sparkling boldness of the whole. This character rises to a climax in the shake towards the end; the shake here becomes the most direct and the most striking expression of the Bacchanalian whirl. The A major, which follows without interposition, has a striking effect, and, like the powerful conclusion, which immediately follows, is a true

Beethoven trait. Particular passages remind us, now and then, of Mozart, but the whole is, as it were, formed in one mould, by some new being, and it seems sometimes, with its Bacchanlian revelry, to foreshadow, though as yet quite faintly, the A major symphony. Lenz says, that the movement is a sort of *rondo à la chasse*, and he perceives the " Halali " quite distinctly. Let him have that as he will; the law of working up the sentiment to a climax is fulfilled in this Sonata by this *finale*. But, I ask again, what has the second movement to do with the organism of the whole ? An inner connection between it and the other moyements is wanting; it belongs to a later stage of development. Lenz seems also to be of this opinion. He somewhat fancifully says that one lingers before the piece as before the Venus of Milo, in the Louvre ; and adds, one would do well to play the movement without the Sonata.

OP. 6, D MAJOR.

Appeared in the winter, 1796-7. Composed, uncertain date.

This is the only Sonata for two performers on the pianoforte which Beethoven has written. It is in the small sonata-form, and is certainly a work of Beethoven's earliest youth, a work which can in no way be compared to the preceding Sonatas, and which is far surpassed even by Mozart's charming little pianoforte duet Sonatas. More cannot be said about this work. It is decidedly doubtful whether

Beethoven had anything to do with its special publication, as op. 6; it is far more likely that some
uncalled-for hand has been at work here.

OP. 7, E FLAT MAJOR.

Appeared in 1797.   *Dedicated to the Countess Babette,
von Keglevics.*

As regards the two first movements this Sonata
is an important one. The first movement, *allegro
molto con brio*, E flat major ⅜ time, is a tone-picture,
rich in colour and character. The aroma of the later
romantic feeling is shed over these tone-pictures;
one has the impression of going into a garden
glittering with a profuse display of the finest and
brightest flowers, all arranged in the most ingenious
manner, so splendidly do the tone-pictures group
themselves and enhance each other's glory. At the
same time, this many coloured play of sounds is
filled with life and soul; that shadow may not be
wanting to the light, a few earnest touches are inter-
spersed here and there, the humorous strains not
being forgotten. This is enough to show the richness of this picture; the reverent player and hearer
will easily feel it all, and the special beauties of the
musical expression will soon reveal themselves.
The second movement, *largo con gran expressione*, C
major, ¾ time, strikes higher chords. The substance
of the movement may be described in a single
word, deep-thoughtfulness (Tiefsinn).. A holy and

exalted tone pervades these strains, which give a glimpse into the depths of the soul. The master seems to have been caught up into higher spheres than those in which he had just lingered. I only say he seems to have been caught up, for he soon feels that a yet higher world lies before him, and a strong yearning after it moves his soul (the motive in A flat major, bar 25). Stronger and stronger becomes the pressure; shattering blows resound on heart and marrow; it is as if fate were knocking at the door, and the soul were reminded of the pain of living by the rough reality of existence. What a powerful, dramatic, agitated passage! The yearning becomes duller, and touching plaintive tones fall on the ear, the mind collects itself into quiet resignation, and, with the return of the first theme, gives itself up again to its first deep reflection and holy meditation (return of the chief theme). Once again is the tone-poet seized with a painful longing after those lighter spheres; but the feeling of what he has been soaring after, of what, in spite of all things, he has won, now takes permanent possession of him, and he rises into a happy trance. With this feeling the movement closes. We find in it what is as yet the most melancholy of *adagii*, for in it real soul-secrets are unveiled; we have the tone-poet Beethoven again with us. In the following movement, Beethoven unfortunately leaves the height to which he had attained. The third movement, *allegro*, E flat major, ¾ time, and *minore* E flat minor certainly is, as regards the latter, with its persistent restless, trills, its harmony and modulations, of a highly original stamp, "a fanciful and plaintive melody, like that of an old German ballad" (Ulibischeff), inclining itself, as Marx says, to an inward, restless, ruminating brooding, being in no way an unworthy successor to the first two movements; but the *allegro*, and especially the fourth movement, *rondo allegretto*, E flat major, ⅔ time, are as regards substance and form, of a strikingly Haydn-Mozartish character, without any prominent originality. They merely present a general indefinite play of sounds, the *finale*, especially, is over-loaded with unattractive figures and passages. The defect of the Sonata throughout is a want of climax; it shows what a deep hold Beethoven's predecessors still had over him. He has only attained a temporary triumph as yet.

OP. 10, No. 1, C MINOR.

Appeared in 1798. Dedicated to the Countess von Browne.

In the succession of the movements this Sonata is characterized by one very steadily developed fundamental thought; it is, however, with the exception, perhaps, of the last movement, written in the Mozart manner. The first movement, *allegro molto*, C minor, ⅔ time, seems as if the composer had been over-hearing his great fore-runner, to whom one might unhesitatingly ascribe the movement, so entirely in Mozart's spirit are the chief themes and their working out. Everything recalls Mozart's great C minor Sonata. The underlying thought of the movement may be called self-contained, restrained passion. Through the second movement, *adagio molto*, A flat major, $\frac{2}{4}$ time, there breathes that Mozartish fervour (Innigkeit), which was not the result of a mental struggle, and which has no such dark back-ground, but rests on the basis of a mind at rest with itself. In correspondence with this is the whole style of the composition, which, without any very special originality in melody, harmony, and modulation, is a reproduction of Mozart, though of course not a slavish but an intelligent one. The difference between Beethoven and Mozart will be fully appreciated by comparing this movement with the *largo* of the previous Sonata, or by playing the two immediately after each other. The conclusion of the movement is very good. The third movement of the Sonata, *prestissimo*, C minor, $\frac{4}{4}$ time, is, on the other hand, the most original. The two chief subjects and their development are quite peculiar, something of the true Beethoven spirit pervades the whole. The master departs from his model and seeks original paths. There is no more reticence or restraint, lively emotion fills the heart, a small battle almost begins; at the same time deeper agitation is entirely wanting. It seems as if the aim of the struggle were to shake off the melancholy character of the minor, the C major

continually breaks through, and is in the end trium-
phant.   One might say, "that's the humour of it."

OP. 10, No. 2, F MAJOR.

Appeared in 1798. *Dedicated to the Countess von Browne.*

In the first and last movements of this Sonata
Beethoven is filled with the spirit of Haydn.   The
jocose, cheerful, easy manner of the merry, roguish
Haydn runs through the first movement, *allegro*, F
major, ¾ time.   The first subject shows this most
strikingly.   It is a delightful *ensemble*, full of diverse
changes, and of surprises, such as the entrance of
the D major, while certain passages bear clear marks
of originality.   But this is all that can be said for
the movement; even the enthusiastic Lenz calls
it meagre.   The second movement, however, *allegro*,
F minor, ¾ time, transports us into Beethoven's
world.   Here are the germs of the Beethoven scherzo;
the master stretches out far beyond the forms of the
Haydn-Mozart minuett, and produces a most original
creation.   The whole is so fantastic, so ætherial,
and has such a magical effect that it awakens in
me a feeling like that of Goethe's words, in "Faust."

> " Wolkenzug und Nebelflor
> Erhellen sich von oben,
> Luft im Laub und Wind im Rohr
> Und Alles ist zerstoben."

Lenz says that it brings before us a Blocken-mountain
scene, from "Faust," while Marx calls attention

to the reposeful harmonies in D flat major, in the middle movement, and justly asks, " Is it, then, only in melody, only in movement, that poetry is to be found?" In the third movement, *prestissimo*, F major, ⅔ time, Beethoven relapses into the style of Haydn. It is constructed on one motive, and pervaded by a Puckish spirit; as Marx observes, a mischievous game between Fugue and Sonata is carried on; the former seeming to resemble an old man with a child pulling his beard.

OP. 10, No. 3, D MAJOR.

Appeared in 1798. *Dedicated to the Countess von Browne.*

In this, which Marx calls the first great Sonata, we clearly recognize the later Beethoven, especially in the first two movements. What spirited, stormy life there is in the first movement, *presto*, D major, ¼ time! How characteristic is the ascent of the first notes in unison from the bass note D to A the fifth above, and then the broken octaves to the tenth above, F sharp, which, by the combination of a descending passage to the fourth A, are rendered still more expressive. The resistless rushing and hurrying depicted in the opening passage are intensified, and there is scarcely a moment of rest; the reposeful motive in A major, in the first part, is powerless to still the raging of the storm. The whole movement is extremely rich

in passages of special beauty.   Particularly noticeable is the masterly power with which the motive,
D, C sharp, B, A, is worked out, the number of
characteristic forms in which it appears, and still
more remarkable is the iron energy displayed in the
fantasia part, and at bar 38, before the conclusion of
the first part, the proudly pacing bass notes and
stormily descending octaves, interwoven with which
is the humorous motive at bar 32—a passage which
re-appears in the third part.   This movement is not
only full of lyric power, but is in the highest degree
dramatic ; it is pervaded by youthful vigour and
heroism ; and, in fancy, we can see, though only
as yet in the dim distance, the creator of the
" Eroica " symphony. The second movement, *largo*,
D minor, $\frac{6}{8}$ time, is a worthy associate of the first.
Marx aptly characterizes its meaning as one of
dismal fretting and depressing melancholy.   It bespeaks deep, manly sorrow born with fortitude ;
in the A major motive the mind finds temporary
rest, only to be speedily overwhelmed with a deep,
impassioned sorrow, which slowly subsides, and
gently dies away.   And now for the musical representation of such a subject !   Does it remind us of
Beethoven's predecessors ?   Not in the least.   Here,
as in the first movement, the whole greatness of the
later Beethoven is already apparent, so new and
original is the composition.   And the dramatic
feeling is again discernible, especially where the
chief subject is heard in the low bass, with a

restless, stormy accompaniment, first in demi-semi-quavers, then in semi-demi-semi-quavers in the treble—a powerful and striking passage! And how well does the thrice-repeated G sharp, shortly before the close, depict the keen, cutting inward woe! This *largo* surpasses any of the slow movements hitherto mentioned, and also many of those in the later Sonatas. Unfortunately, the other parts of the Sonata are not up to the level of the two first movements. The third movement, *minuetto*, D major, $\frac{3}{4}$ time, sunnily bright as it and the teasing G major trio both are, does not accord well with the unfathomable depths of sorrow of the *largo*. Marx, however, thinks differently, and considers the movement as a correct and necessary member in the organism of the piece (compare his " Composition-slehre," part 3). Supposing that in the inward, as in the outward world, there is a refreshing sunshine clearing up all the mysteries of darkness, and granting that psychological correctness requires that brightness and light should follow the night which had gathered round the *largo*, still it seems to me that the movement in question has too much of that light Haydnish cheerfulness, I might say too little of the ideality of form which was peculiar to Beethoven, when in a bright humour and quite himself, to be considered as in clear and necessary connection with the previous movements. I always have the impression that Beethoven lost his cue here ; I miss the working up of the ruling thought.

Nor does the fourth movement, *rondo allegro*, D major, ⁴ time, supply this want. It certainly is more characteristic than the third movement ; the first motive is original and worked out into the most diverse forms, in a masterly manner, while the whole is exceedingly lively and not without humour. But the influence of Beethoven's predecessors is apparent at intervals, which in the *largo* was slightly perceptible, and in the first movement scarcely at all. After the depth and grandeur of the two first movements, the tone and keeping of the whole of this movement appears to me too light and fleeting, and the humour too shallow, to give an impression of any striking internal unity, or to form an adequate conclusion of the whole work.

OP. 13, C MINOR.

Appeared, 1799. *Dedicated to Prince Lichnowsky.*

In this Sonata Beethoven again attains a very close unity in the individual movement. The work has always enjoyed a special preference among *dilettanti*. It may be described as one of the master's most popular compositions, and is the *ne plus ultra* with those who have not arrived at an understanding of the later works, such as Op. 57. The name " Pathétique " may have contributed to this, as has also the fact that the Sonata is easy to play, more easy than, for example, the last named work. But the intellectual nature of the work, the plastic

emotional images, explain the preference ; the Sonata
comes very near to the emotional understanding,
and the title " Pathétique " is striking and not
easily mistaken, although other works are equally
if not more pathetic.   Here the pathos is deep,
earnest passion, which, however, does not over-step
a certain measure of gravity, and is accompanied
with a dignified deportment.   The first movement,
grave, then *allegro molto con brio*, C minor, $\frac{4}{4}$ time,
is the most telling expression of this primary character, a life-like picture of manly, earnest, painfully
stirred passion.   In the weighty introduction the
ardour seems restrained ;   here and there the fire
already breaks out, in a marked rhythm, but only to
be immediately quenched.   At the entrance of the
allegro, however, the lava stream bursts its bounds,
and pours forth broadly.   In the tributary subject,
in E flat minor, and then more deeply and intensely
in D flat major, a pleading, soothing voice is heard
within restraining the storm.   But in vain is the
stream dammed.   A moment's rest is perceptible
in the passage marked *grave*.   Then the storm
begins anew and with increased power in E minor.
And again arise those beseeching, soothing strains
in F minor and C minor.   But in vain ; the storm
must spend its fury, till at length it subsides in
a diminished chord of the seventh.   A third time
the *grave* appears, and then a last short outburst,
followed by deep repose.   Marx mentions the repeated appearance of the *grave* as particularly

significant. Says he: "It does not stand there as an empty clang of sounds or chords, but has its own especial purpose in the mind of the composer, and is in accordance with the character and thought of the whole; three times before the end it solemnly points back to the heavy approach to the work." The nature of this *grave* gives the impression that it could be the product only of some strong determination. After the sharp struggle, the master's mind is filled with the deepest, soul-felt peace; in the second movement, *adagio cantabile*, A flat major, ⅜ time, a chord is struck, of which a sustained singing theme is the most direct expression. The feeling becomes more and more deep and holy, and rises, in the end, to real rapture. Once only, when the theme is heard in A flat minor, a deep sorrow breaks through; this produces courageous, joyful exaltation (transition to E major); a moment, and the untroubled forms of rest and peace again close around us. The third movement, *rondo allegro*, C minor, ¼ time, is the adjusting conclusion of the whole. The storm, which swept through the soul in the first movement, has subsided, the tone-poet has saved and secured his inward peace; his mind has, in a measure, purified itself. The *finale* seems the result of this purifying process—its most direct expression. More strictly speaking, the result is a certain submission to something that was inevitable, but a happy, courageous submission, full of power for fresh exertions, and renewed activity.

There runs also through this movement an active, though not unquiet, flow of life in many changing forms, " bewegt und doch massvoll Alles,"—an agreeable conclusion. It is not to be denied that the last movement, both in its chief subject and in other particulars of its formal construction, reminds one very much of Mozart, far more so than does the *finale* of the previous Sonata.

OP. 14, Nos. 1 and 2, E MAJOR, and G MAJOR.

Appeared, 1799; when composed, uncertain. Dedicated to the Baroness Braun.

After the D major Sonata, Op. 6, these Sonatas are the weakest of the works yet mentioned, and are very inferior to Op. 2.

The whole of the second Sonata, particularly, might be unhesitatingly ascribed to Haydn, while the first is a little more independent, but so little that, although it would do honour to the pupil, it does none to the master. Through Schindler, these Sonatas have received what one might almost call an undeserved celebrity; at any rate, one which Beethoven did not anticipate. Schindler makes mention, in his Biography of Beethoven, of a conversation with him, in the year 1823, in which Beethoven described the contents of the Sonatas as a dialogue between man and wife, or between lover and mistress, as the conflict of two principles. Marx, in his work on Beethoven, takes much trouble to place the purport and importance of this speech in a right light; that is, to reduce it to proper proportions. We quite agree with him that Beethoven's expression had no special reference to the works in question. Indeed, all instrumental music contains contrasts, like the image of the man and woman; conflicting principles, such as are frequently found in Haydn and Mozart: in an æsthetic point of view, therefore, the expression proves nothing or too much, for Beethoven has, in other works, composed more clever dialogues. In these Sonatas one can imagine a conversation between man and wife, but it does not place them in a more important light. Besides, Marx fully shows that they really do not contain the least trace of dialogues. Like Marx, we may find these Sonatas attractive and very agreeable, but for Beethoven we seek in vain. Their meaning is so obvious, the feelings which they depict are so simple and clear, that a further explanation would be superfluous.

OP. 22, B FLAT MAJOR.

Composed, 1800.   *Dedicated to the Count von Browne.*

In the two first movements of this Sonata deeper chords are again struck. The first movement, *allegro con brio*, B flat major, $\frac{4}{4}$ time, is remarkable for energy and strong youthful activity; a fresh pulse of life beats through these tones, a joyful, courageous feeling pervades the whole. Very characteristic is the first theme; it gives the signal for action, and, in passages of highly-coloured tone-painting, a very brisk movement is depicted, which is inter-rupted only by the firm, courageous entry of the second subject in thirds and sixths. Towards the end of the first part, there is a third motive in octaves, majestically rising and falling, and having the appearance of an earnest, manly form in the midst of a gay, youthful crowd. With the second part a new and characteristic movement begins. It appears, at first, like some strange apparition whose entrance causes a precipitate retreat among the surrounding elements; but the scattered forms gradually re-unite, the treble performing passages of rapidly-rolling semi-quavers, while the bass moves to and fro in crotchets and quavers; after which comes a momentary pause. In the third part, with the return of the chief theme, the former chequered movement recommences, as if the composer wished to be serious once more before he concluded, although only for an instant. In some parts of the movement we are still reminded of Mozart, but, in general, Beethoven's originality decidedly appears. As much cannot be said for the second movement, *adagio*, E flat maior, $\frac{2}{4}$ time. A deep yearning breathes through the first theme, a pleasant calm and a peculiar romantic feeling pervade the entire movement; but, at the same time, the whole seems somewhat weak; it might be said that the melody was tinged with the lusciousness of the best kind of Italian music, and thus seemed foreign to the Beethoven of our imagination. Although this movement is no improvement on the first, it is not inferior to it, as the two last movements unfortunately are. Beethoven decidedly relapses into the Haydn-Mozart style of writing both in the third movement, *minuett*, B flat major, ¾ time, and also in the fourth, *rondo allegretto*, B flat major, ¾ time. A general, cheerful tone of feeling, wanting in individual expression, runs through both these movements ; and they have but little originality.

OP. 26, A FLAT MAJOR.

Composed, 1801.   *Dedicated to Prince Lichnowsky.*

Compared with previous works, this Sonata is remarkable as being the first example of Beethoven's use of the variation and march forms. Indeed the work is not written in the true Sonata form, for it consists of an air with variations, a minuett, and a funeral march, concluding with a rondo. The Sonata fails in organic unity, owing to the interpolation of the march, which, although a masterly work of musical art, and a worthy predecessor to the funeral march of the " Eroica " Symphony, seems as if it were " stuck into " this Sonata. It would be useless to seek for any connection between it and the other movements. How does it agree with the fugitive character of the concluding movement, causing it to sound thin and weak after the depth and grandeur of the march, and producing an effect which dispels all the enchant-

ment of the slow movement? The concluding
rondo is the weakest part of the whole. But in
proportion to its inferiority is the superiority
and beauty of the air with variations. This theme
breathes an ardent longing, arising, as Marx says,
out of a deep, yearning, exalted feeling. "In the
glorious variations," says Marx, "this fervent feeling
is fully developed; it creates the variations. The
first notes E, A flat, inspired with this higher meaning, become the motive of the first variation; the
feeling increases and is diversified at every step,
when the longed-for motive is worked up higher
and higher, till, in the fourth octave from the beginning, it sinks back timidly and reservedly into its
native regions. Everything is resolved into motion
in the second variation, in which the appearance
of the theme in the tenor serves to intensify the
conflict of emotions. The same impulse, though
in a more fretful tone, influences the following
variation, whence it naturally results that a gentle
spirit of consolation, now sinking, now soaring,
hovers over the next variation. The last variation
gives the theme divided alternately between the
soprano and alto, in an agitated but still a more
confident manner, and finishes with a sweet pleasing
hushing." Beethoven treats the variation form in
a totally different manner from Mozart, for example.
The latter constructs his variation merely on the
formal musical foundation of the theme; with him
the variation is more like an ingenious paraphrase

of the form of the theme, but with Beethoven the intellectual side of the theme and the nature of its sentiment, becomes the ruling motive for each variation, so that a greater internal transformation is observable. But only in the later works does this principle appear quite clearly. The *scherzo* of this Sonata, and the *trio* especially, are not devoid of considerable originality ; the latter is, as Marx says, " one of those gently-breathing, self-reposeful sort of trios, such as Beethoven alone could write."

OP. 27, No. 1, E FLAT MAJOR.

Composed about 1801. *Dedicated to Princess Liechtenstein.*

This Sonata is entitled, " *sonata quasi una fantasia,*" and, both in form and matter, it is more like a fantasia than a Sonata. The strict and true Sonata form is almost entirely put aside, and the whole seems to me like a mixture of song, rondo, fantasia, and Sonata, for all these forms enter into it, and in such a manner that they all have equal prominence. There is, in consequence, a want of unity both of sentiment and form, an air of incongruity, an abrupt transition from motive to motive, characteristic of the free fantasia, and a visible striving after a decided individual nature. The movements seem very slightly connected, and there is a fragmentary character about the work as if it were an experiment in form. The first movement, *andante*, E flat major, $\frac{4}{4}$ time, with an interlude, *allegro*, C major, $\frac{6}{8}$ time, is written in the romantic style, after the manner of a song. The constant return of the theme, good as it may in itself be, gives rise to a certain monotony, while the absence of orchestral colouring precludes variety. But what shall be said of the jovial interlude? How does it accord with the elegiac tone of the principal part? It may be called Beethoven's humour; but to my mind it does not seem in keeping here. Whatever were Beethoven's intentions, they were not realized. And this is the case also with the incessant repetition of the chief subject which we have already noticed. One can only compare it with the second movement of Op. 90. The second movement, *allegro molto vivace*, C minor, ¾ time, is not devoid of originality, with its rash, unstable, hurrying character, and, in its humour, it already clearly bears the stamp of the Beethoven *scherzo*. The third movement, *adagio*, A flat major, ¾ time, is of the true Beethoven cast, displaying depth and warmth of feeling. The movement is astonishingly short and original, more like an introduction to the last, fourth movement, *allegro vivace*, E flat major, ¾ time—a bright, lively, agitated composition, with a dash of fantasy, almost of elfishness.

OP. 27, No. 2, C SHARP MINOR.

Composed about 1801.
Dedicated to the Countess Julie Guicciardi.

This Sonata is undoubtedly one of the greatest and most important productions, not only in the circle of the Sonata, but in the whole of Beethoven's instrumental music.   This work, to which the mark *quasi fantasia* has also been attached, enjoys, in another manner, the same favour as Op. 13.   Disappointed affection was the moving cause for this Sonata, which is dedicated " Alla Damigella Giulietta Guicciardi." " Beethoven shows," says Marx, " in his immortal C sharp minor Sonata, that love—a secret flame burning itself out in the consuming fire of insatiable desire—lived on in his true heart."   Marx describes the first movement, *adagio*, C sharp minor, ¢ time, as the song of renunciation.   We hear soft, deep, plaintive tones, such as arise from the troubled and oppressed heart.   The bitter pain reaches a climax in the characteristic chords of the ninth in bars 16, 18, 52, 54; but closely blended with this heart-trouble is a feeling of quiet submission to the inevitable, and occasionally—the change into the major key—a comforting ray of light enters into the night.   With melancholy and pain the movement began, and with these it dies away.   The musical colouring is bewitching, a strange dim light is shed over the whole, and yet amid all the darkness and confusion a definite sentiment is preserved.   An *allegretto*, D flat major, ¾ time, follows as the second movement.   Marx says : " The song of renunciation is followed by the parting, 'Oh, think of me! I think of thee! Farewell, farewell!' uttered in fleeting, broken, and lamenting tones, till the last 'for ever.' Who shall pourtray the pictures of happy moments gone by, or the shadows of a dark future which hover around the spirit of the resigned one in the trio?" This is an ingenious interpretation of the movement which Liszt, looking at the crashing movement that follows, calls a floweret between two abysses. But I confess, frankly, that this *allegretto*, with regard to the style in which it is written, the character which pervades it, and the connection in which it stands, always seems to me like an interloper. Is this really Beethoven's own style, or is it that of the Haydn-Mozart Minuett? This *allegretto* always puts me into a mood which seems the result of totally different feelings to those which pervade the rest of the Sonata. I feel a shock to my feelings in being suddenly snatched from the poetic spell of the *adagio*, and transported from the profoundest soul-depths into a light, fleeting, easy-going sort of world. I may be mistaken, so I will not seek to spoil any one else's enjoyment of this *allegretto ;* to me, however, it is a mystery in this place, which Marx even cannot explain. In the last movement, *presto agitato*, C sharp minor, ⁴₄ time, the temper of the tone-poet bursts forth in gloomy passionate agitation, the pent-up wrath breaks boldly into free channels, a frightful storm begins to rage, as if some volcano were pouring forth glowing lava from its thundering depths, and dark spirits arise and close around us. Could this be better represented than in the opening motive, and in the train of the wildest harmonies and modulations which surge like billowy

waves of the sea? The sublime spectacle of the
giant's struggle with these powers of darkness is
displayed before us. Will the struggler succumb?
' No,' says the second subject, that strong confident
form, which appears first at bar 21, and ' No,' says
also that flash of free humour in A Major, in bar 33,
and afterwards in D major. Such power the spirits
have not attained to, and there are hopeful flashes of
light in the chaos. The storm may rage till the
end; but it has then worn itself out, and the soul is
purified, freed, and saved. Such is the indelible
ideal meaning of this incomparably richly coloured
night piece, and we part from the work with the
happy consciousness of having listened to some of
the truest tone-poetry.

OP. 28, D MAJOR.

Composed, 1801. *Dedicated to Joseph Edlen
von Sonnenfels.*

The title " Pastorale " has been given to this
Sonata. Marx expatiates on this in an ironical
manner, and, pointing to the Pastoral Symphony,
thinks that in Beethoven's works, which bear this
name aright, there is not a single repetition of a
fundamental thought to be found. We cannot subscribe to this opinion, which is only true in a certain
sense, and must be taken *cum grano salis.* To me,
the Sonata, at any rate, always recalls feelings akin
to those which we perceive in works like the Pastoral

Symphony. And does not a gentle fresh spring-breeze breathe through the first movement, *allegro*, D major, ⅜ time? This is indeed a sunny-bright and intelligent picture of life, pleasing, richly coloured, and full of charming changes. We feel that it does not exhaust the full meaning of the movement, and that a deeper sense lies in the whole ; but the interpretation which Marx (Beethoven, vol. i. page 311, first edition) gives to the movement, and to the whole Sonata, seems to me rather a forced one. We agree with him, "that a hidden meaning seems to run through" the first movement. The succession of harmonies and the modulations have often a wonderful effect. Take, for instance, only the *point d'orgue* on the low F sharp, in the so-called fantasia-part ; truly, "thousands cannot comprehend it." This first movement is purely Beethovenish ; not so the following ones. The second movement, *andante*, D minor, ⅜ time, produces a feeling like that which comes over us when light veils of cloud darken the sun, making a beautiful landscape shine in fallow light, the cloud only breaking a little now and then for the friendly sunbeams to fall through. The third movement, *scherzo allegro vivace*, D major, ⅜ time, is full of a gay, teasing humour, characteristic through the succession of octaves, thirds, sixths, and triads, and the *trio* again is not without originality in its obstinate repetition of a single motive. The movement is only a play of sounds, and, however good a one, is not a tone-poem like the first movement.

This may be said also of the fourth movement, *rondo allegro ma non troppo*, D major, $\frac{2}{4}$ time. We seem to see before us a troop of lusty sons of nature wantonly jesting, springing and romping, seizing each other and running away, playing hide and seek, keeping as still as mice, and then bursting out and running on more and more joyfully and wildly. Haydn and Mozart appear very clearly—too clearly—in these last three movements, and this is one reason why an inequality in style clings to this Sonata also, and the working up of the primary thought is wanting. The work always seems to me like a Janus with two heads—the one turned backwards, the other forwards.

OP. 31, No. 1, G MAJOR.

Composed about 1802.

Humour, grace, and comfort are the three general characteristics of the three movements of this Sonata. Marx briefly and pertinently describes the first movement, *allegro vivace*, G major, $\frac{2}{4}$ time, as ingenious and sparkling with humour. The short chief subject has a striking effect with its strongly marked rhythm, and the rhythmical form implied by this motive gives to the Sonata its special originality. A fine contrast is afforded by the second theme, which, full of a comfortable enjoyment, enters first in B major, and also by a third motive of a similar character, which is heard towards the end of the first part in the same key, and afterwards in G major. The whole movement is rich in surprising changes, in the bold management of the melody, harmony, and modulation, and is thus highly interesting and lively. The second movement, *adagio grazioso*, C major, ⅜ time, is a picture of refined, sweet smiling gracefulness; Marx and Lenz are right in calling it idealised Italian music. In fact, Beethoven lavishly displays all sorts of sensuous charms; and yet he never loses himself in effeminacy and flabby sentiment; never forgets that he is a German, and breathes German sincerity even into these strains. This is especially apparent in the tributary subject in A flat *pp.*, in which the master, with quiet, magical power, tears us away from the laughing Hesperides, and leads us here, and also in the clever conclusion of the movement, into the depths of German feeling. The third movement, *rondo allegretto*, G major, ¼ time, belongs to the easy-going type. Nothing could be more characteristic in this respect than the first subject. This theme dominates the whole of the very long movement, of which Marx says that it is possessed exclusively by a comfortable jog-trot spirit. The theme is presented in all possible changes, exhibiting inexhaustible ingenuity. But I think he has done too much in this respect, and has not been able to prevent a certain formality from pervading the whole. This arises from the motive itself, which does not seem to me capable and worthy of a rich and interesting treatment. I think, too, that the

E

composer felt this himself eventually, for, towards the end, he suddenly brings in an *adagio*, and then closes as suddenly with a short *presto*, which is in some measure a pleasant and refreshing change. Moreover, comfortableness is, so to speak, something quite un-Beethovenish. Closely observed, the chief subject of the third movement, and several motives also of the previous movements, are rather Mozartish in invention. Altogether it conclusively appears that this Sonata, no less than its predecessors, fails in the working up of the primary thought.

OP. 31, No. 2, D MINOR.

Composed about 1802.

The first movement of this Sonata, *allegro*, D minor, ¢ time, is a dramatic picture of a manly, earnest, passionate and powerful conflict, accompanied by inward struggles. In the beginning of the movement, the master still betrays indecision; he pauses, reflecting whether he shall take the decisive step or not. After one essay, however, he decides, and the storm bursts in; at bar 21 the chief theme comes out with, as Marx says, stern decision and full force, which, however, joins itself to a gentler impulse of pain or of supplication; the feeling becomes more and more restless, and the second theme has a very agitated character. Now some hard blows resound as if the struggling spirit were bracing itself for fresh efforts. Then the

deep, discontented mutterings and rollings re-com-
mence. At the beginning of the second part we
hear again the *largo* tones; "the *largo* question
sounds solemnly three times," and the responses
are more eager aspirations and passionate struggles.
A moment's rest comes again, the *largo* is heard
once more in a recitative full of expression, and
of sorrowful submission to the inevitable. Such
I take to be the meaning of the recitative. Then
the struggling and striving are renewed, till at last
the storm subsides and dies away in dull, deep
mutterings. The second movement, *adagio*, B flat
major, ⅜ time, depicts the deepest peace and sweetest
happiness. A religious feeling pervades the chief
theme of this movement. But amid all this repose
come occasional outbursts of violent agitation; unspeakable feelings rise and swell in the heart; an
ardent yearning after higher happiness takes possession of the soul, the impulse is gently silenced,
but again begins the yearning, which is, however,
quieted at last. The whole is a beautiful and richly
coloured piece of soul-painting. The third movement,
allegretto, D minor, ⅜ time, consists properly of only
two principal subjects; the first quite at the beginning of the movement of four notes only, A, F, E, D;
the second of six notes at the interval of a second
(F, E, F, E, F, E.) This gives a stamp of originality to the piece, especially in the second tune-
less motive, and something of a *bizarre* tinge is
imparted by the almost obstinate repetition of the

theme in every key. What does this movement mean ?
A deep agitation runs through it; we see a striving
after something, similar to that in the first movement,
only not so strong; I might say a more resigned
striving which seems, however, to be accompanied
by a sharp, almost gnawing sorrow. Over the whole,
which Marx aptly calls "perfumed with longing,"
there breathes a fanciful spirit; a humorous feature
runs through it, by which the former restless, even
gloomy, character of the movement is essentially
modified. We feel convinced, on careful consideration, that this *rondo* is no mere caprice, and that
there is, although we may not be able to explain
how, a delicate connection between it and the first
movement. And the Sonata on this account gives
the impression of a work uniformly carried out.
It may also be noticed that, according to tradition,
Beethoven had a special preference for this Sonata,
and frequently played it in public.

OP. 31, No. 3, E FLAT MAJOR.

Composed about 1802.

The first movement, *allegro* E flat major, $\frac{3}{4}$ time,
begins with a short characteristic motive, such as
has already appeared in the last named Sonata,
and which we shall meet with again in the following
works. The first subject has a playful, humorous
stamp, and, as it is elaborated, its facetious character
predominates more and more, especially at the begin-

ning of the second part, where, now in the treble, now in the bass, it skips about in a charming elfish manner. The movement is formed also on a second theme which first appears in B flat major, then in E flat major. Although the first motive was very original, this has a decidedly Mozartish colouring, which shows itself also in the further development of the piece. In this movement, the independent Beethoven is quite clearly distinguishable from the Beethoven leaning towards Mozart. The former meets us again in the second movement, *scherzo allegro vivace*, A flat major, $\frac{2}{4}$ time. This is one of the sweetest and most ætherial movements Beethoven ever wrote. One fancies one's self transported into the fantastic and humorous elfin world, into a scene in the "Midsummer Night's Dream," so magical is the spirit which pervades the composition. The charm of the colouring, the splendid and surprising effect of the alternation of *forte* and *piano*, especially the *ff* in F major, afterwards in D flat major, is indescribable. This movement is true fairy work. The third movement, *menuetto moderato et grazioso*, E flat major, $\frac{3}{4}$ time, strongly reminds us of Mozart, so entirely is it conceived in his spirit; the *trio*, however, shows far more Beethovenish originality. This may be said also of the last movement, *presto con fuoco*, E flat major, $\frac{6}{8}$ time, in which the climax of the ruling humorous spirit of the whole Sonata is reached. This *finale* is formed on two short characteristic motives, one at the beginning of the movement, the other at the twelfth bar, both of which are, the latter especially, carried out in the most surprising and diversified manner. The climax is reached in the second part, where, by an enharmonic change of the G flat, F sharp major is introduced, and is further modulated into G major, the humour thus boldly and brightly expressing itself. The whole Sonata is one of the most cheerful and most free from pain which Beethoven has written; the utmost frolicksomeness and a sparkling delight in life—such, in short, is the character of the work.

OP. 49, No. 1, G MINOR, No. 2, G MAJOR.

Composed about 1802.

There is but little to be said about these Sonatas. They are properly sonatinas, like Op. 6; though they are deeper than Op. 14. They are undoubtedly productions of Beethoven's earliest youth, and for their taking rank as Op. 49 the composer is least of all answerable. All that is noticeable is that the motive of the minuett in the second Sonata had already appeared in the Septuor, Op. 20. This circumstance would indicate an earlier origin for the Sonatas, for it is hardly conceivable of Beethoven that he should afterwards have worked out, in such narrow limits, a motive from one of his most important works of the first period. The connection existing here is similar to that between the first theme of the last movement of the *eroica* and the pianoforte variations on it, and in another sense between the singing-theme in the Fantasia, Op. 80, and the song of joy in the ninth Symphony; that is, a sort of preliminary study is afforded us.

OP. 53, C MAJOR.

Composed about 1803. *Appeared in* 1805. *Dedicated to Count Waldstein.*

What a giant Beethoven is in this Sonata! The first movement, *allegro con brio*, C major, ¢ time, begins with gentle tremblings of the happiest feeling in the tone depths, embodied in a short characteristic motive. An upward impulse towards the light makes itself felt. For a moment the happy beating of the heart finds rest on a close in G. But it immediately begins again more intensely under the firm keeping of the chief motive, and passes through a short tributary movement to the second theme in the bright E major. This theme, which, in contrast to the previous trembling feelings, has a firm self-contained character, produces a delicious effect. So alluring is the spell of this motive that a host of charming forms immediately surround it. The tone-poet's soul is filled with the happiest, sweetest self-forgetfulness, quite given up to this beguiling play, absorbed, as it were, in this fairy world. Will it entirely lose itself? No. At the entrance of the

A major, a manly self-reliant power is perceptible which, in F major, rises to a bold shout of triumph, but only to sink back again into the first delicious trembling, and then instantly to hush the most pleasing emotions till the end of the first part. With the second part that electric spark of joy in the first theme flashes forth again, and is exclusively employed in the fantasia part, till, in C major, those bright genii again flit around the soul with more power than ever, bringing in the third part and the return to the first theme, with the recurrence of the same train of feelings that we had in the first part. At the entrance of the Coda, the first theme appears in the greatest intensity, the happy feeling rises to a magnificent climax, till the agitation checks itself with the chord of the dominant seventh. The light, self-contented form of the second theme is heard once again in the quiet depth, then another outburst of the electrical first motive, followed by rolling thunder and—all is silent. If we now examine in detail the musical structure of this movement, we shall be astonished at the wealth of means employed, at the inexhaustibleness of the master in ever new harmonic and rhythmical changes; in a word, at the gigantic structure which he has reared on those two motives. Thus in the Coda especially, all possible harmonic and rhythmical means are applied to intensify the sentiment to the utmost. There follows, as a second movement, *introduzione adagio molto*, F major, $\frac{3}{4}$ time, with rondo *allegretto moderato*,

C major, ¾ time.* The slow introduction has an
aphoristic fragmentary character, and, with the
exception of eight bars in the middle, which contain
a deep, yearning motive, it consists, so to speak, of
musical interrogations, and bold, harmonious, even
mystical changes, which lead to the rondo. The
adagio, which Marx calls meditative, forms a striking
contrast to the happy character of the preceding
and following movements, and thus enhances their
vivacity; so pale is the colouring that it seems as if
the smiling face of the heavens were suddenly
covered with the shadows of mist and cloud. Then
the mists suddenly disperse, the brightest sunshine
comes back again, when the chief theme of the rondo
is heard. This motive is thoroughly imbued with
the blissful spirit of the second theme in the first
movement, it is at the same time very homely and
simple, and even naïvely popular. This melody
constantly returns, and so firm is its hold that it
springs up ever anew, with fresh harmonic and
rhythmical embellishments, always the same yet
ever in a fresh dress, like the former theme surrounded with delicate charming forms. Suddenly
there appears, in a rolling trilling movement, a
strong, manly power, revealing a flood of feeling
which rises even to a certain gloomy bitterness

---

* According to Ries, the "Andante favori pour piano,"
No. 35 of the works which have no opus numbers was originally
to have formed the second (middle) movement.

(A minor). Who can explain what it is that suddenly, almost painfully, agitates the soul? Albeit, the night is but short, for the tender blissful feeling of the first theme soon comes out victoriously. Once more a violent storm arises in C minor, dark shadows close around the scene, but they also vanish. The chief theme appears again in a shortened form but in the utmost intensity, the expression almost rises to sublimity; a moment and the earnest feeling passes away in enchanting modulations, in the happiest gentleness, and then in real ecstacy. This feeling reaches its first climax in G flat and D·flat major, from which a musing train of feeling leads back to the fundamental thought. The chief theme grows more and more striking and expressive up till the arrival of the marvellous climax with the merry trills. This is the second climax of joyful ecstacy, the third and highest being attained in the celebrated chain trills of the *prestissimo* which afford the clearest, sharpest, most striking, and most effective expression of the fundamental thought. Here is the fulfilment of what was only sought after in the C major Sonata, Op. 2, for what was only bud there is now developed into the finest blossom.

Op. 54, F MAJOR.

Composed about 1803.

This Sonata is one of Beethoven's most singular works. Marx calls it a strange production, and apparently does not very well know what to say about it ; he considers it as a mere play of sounds, not as music of the soul, much less of the intellect, in which categories—(to these we shall return)—he arranges instrumental music. Lens finds the Sonata *bizarre* only, and sees in it the weak side merely of the Third Period without its beauties. I must confess that the work is a mystery to me also. I look upon it as a freak of Beethoven's. The first movement, *tempo di minuetto*, F major, ¾ time, contains two chief themes, the first is of the quiet, cheerful, comfortable stamp, the second, a series of octaves rushing to and fro, is rather dry and has no charm of melody. The two alternating motives run side by side without uniting organically to form a higher whole ; they seem as if they had nothing to do with each other, so entirely does each pursue its own way. If there is a leading thought at all, what is it ? Solve the riddle who can. The movement remains an enigma to me. The second movement, *allegro*, F major, ¾ time, appears to me one of the weakest which Beethoven has ever written. Is this to be the Third Period ? The movement consists of mere figure work ; it seems to me empty and insignificant ; at the most, valuable as a study. The whole work falls coldly. The saying that " even Homer nods sometimes " hits the mark exactly, for the work shows no signs of inspiration. It must be observed, however, that, according to Schindler, this Sonata, which was printed in 1806, was written, several years before Op. 47.

Composed, 1804. Dedicated to Count Brunswick.

The title, *Appassionata,* which has been given to this Sonata, seems nothing less than exhaustive of its rich contents. In the first and third movements the work is a night piece, a picture of a violent emotional conflict, illuminated, however, by flashes of humour; the middle movement is an ideal flight into happier regions. The first movement, *allegro assai,* F minor, ¹²⁄₈ time, begins with one of those short characteristic themes, such as we have already frequently met with; dismal spectral shadows rise, as it were, out of the lowest depths; soft wailings issue from the heart, and fate is heard knocking at the door. Suddenly a mighty storm bursts forth, then there is a painful trembling, and in the second theme in A flat major, there arises a wonderful sympathetic strain of happy consolation. The storm of painful passion begins again, the first flashes of humour disappear, the movement takes the form of convulsive startings, the nightly shadows assume a firmer shape, the inward commotion increases, until the return of another outburst of humour. Now, everything is momentarily stilled into soft trembling tones, and that spirit of strong, manly, exalted consolation gains the upper hand. But fate claims its rights, the fight must be fought out, so

the turmoil begins again. Although the voice of
consolation is heard for the third time, the storm
only rages the more vehemently; although a comforting ray of light descends from above, an almost
horrible shrillness resounds from below; at the
entrance of the broken chord the inward struggle
rises to actual frenzy; there is a restless surging
to and fro, the consoling motive even takes a gloomy
character, and at last the roaring thunder rolls.
We have here again a thoroughly dramatic psychological picture, and the feelings that pervade it are
real, heart-felt experiences. The second movement,
adante con moto, D flat major, ⅜ time, comes as a
contrast between the beginning and concluding
movements, though not outwardly, but deeply and
inwardly: it is a steadfast island between two
agitated oceans. From the quiet depths there arises
a holy song of blessed peace; "a fervent prayer,
does this theme seem, standing firmly in the low
dark depths, closely compact, full of longing, like
a prayer out of the profoundest darkness" *(Marx)*.
This melody is a sunbeam full of refreshing warmth,
flooding the innermost recesses of the soul, full
of unending charm. How well is the soothing, pain
and woe-relieving character of the melody expressed
in the modulation from the sixth to the seventh bars
of the first strophe; and then, in the second strophe,
what a blissful glimpse of heaven, what quiet, happy
confidence! Most charming is the variation of the
theme. The different variations are not dependent

on the formal musical structure of the theme; the changes are the result of the ideal contents: this determines each variation. The nature of the first variation is, as Marx puts it, shy, the theme is only repeated timidly, the melody is broken, the bass drags slowly but closely after it. In the second variation, the song becomes more agitated and is heard in a higher, brighter octave. In the third variation the expression of the theme, which is, as it were, surrounded by an accompaniment of harps, rises to pure ecstacy, the soul seems lifted from earth, enveloped in the blue boundless vault of heaven. But we soon return to earth; the theme is heard again in its first simplicity; at last it is silent, and painful strains forebode the storm of the *finale.* Marx describes the whole *andante* as a prayer full of comfort, arising out of the deepest desolation. The third movement, *allegro ma non troppo*, F minor, ⁹⁄₈ time, begins with a number of sixths, resembling a wild outcry from a soul filled with anguish, then a sweeping movement in the bass, like a wild mountain torrent rushing foaming down. It frets and fumes, till a clear, firm form struggles out of the whirl, rushes in with wild passion, accompanied by plaintive thirds ("the storm song"), the agitation ever increasing till the conclusion of the first part. The roar of the soul's storm is renewed at the entrance of the second part, sparks of humour soon flash forth again, and then a short tributary motive bespeaks deep inward trouble. Now there is a distant, restless surging, a mighty rolling in the depths; then the struggle becomes a little quieter, a wild whirl of octaves in C major leads to some peculiar convulsive startings which, at length, exhaust themselves; and, in characteristic minims, bring in a momentary dead silence. But only momentary; for, at the beginning of the third part, the storm renews itself, the gloomy spectacle of the first part is repeated, and isolated flashes of humour dart across the night. At last, in the *presto*, the tone-poet comes forth like a warrior in steel harness, and, with proud manly grandeur, seems to say, in the full chords, " Behold! the storm has not broken the oak; it approaches again, but it will not break it." A final storm indeed follows, but it is powerless; the spirit has freed itself, and at last the struggle ceases in solemn minor tones. We have the assurance that the tone-poet has not succumbed to the powers of evil; he has but tried and tempted his moral, manly power in the conflict. A *gloria* song of triumph at the end would correspond to the idea of the work; the conclusion must have an earnest tragical exaltation, as the work generally may be called an emotional tragedy. Besides, according to Ries, the conception of this *finale* is a stormy night, and when Beethoven was asked by Schindler for a key to this work, and to the D minor Sonata, Op. 31, he replied: " Read Shakespeare's *Tempest.*" We ask, also, with Marx, what has that to do with it ? Nothing less than finding the key to it. It is true, as Marx says, that much of what is called fantasy is to be found in this work, especially in the first movement; but we must add that it is a fantasy bounded and governed by reason and force of will, a fantasy in which are represented all the never-ending depths of the human heart.

OP. 78, F SHARP, MAJOR.

Appeared, 1798. Dedicated to the Countess von Brunswick.

The first movement, *adagio cantabile*, and *allegro ma non troppo*, F sharp major, $\frac{2}{4}$ time and $\frac{4}{4}$ time, begins with a motive full of deep yearning, is truly Beethovenish, as is the chief theme of the *allegro* which follows it. But the continuation does not fulfil the expectations that we have raised, for the movement loses in substance, and fritters itself away in a play of sounds devoid of any deeper meaning. Still more decidedly is this the case with the second movement, *allegro vivace*, F sharp major, $\frac{2}{4}$ time. It is needless to waste many words over this when we are still full of the impression left by the F minor Sonata. Marx even passes over this Sonata in silence, and Lenz says, simply and pertinently, "Beethoven's hand has worked at it, but not his genius."

OP. 79, G MAJOR.

Appeared, 1810. Date uncertain when composed.

The above remark is still more decidedly applicable to this Sonatina, as the work is called. It is without doubt a youthful production, like the Sonatas, Op. 49. The opus number, 79, has neither rhyme nor reason. One would rather have supposed Haydn to be the composer, had not Beethoven been named as such. The work must surely have been published afterwards as a stop-gap. For the use and edification of those who are interested even in this trifle of the great Beethoven, we will again quote Marx, who says the Sonatina presents a "*presto alla tedesca*," superficial but lively, (if only the modulation of the cuckoo-like concluding movement in the second part were not far too tame) a small, essentially small *andante* G minor, and a Viennese-like joyful *finale*.

OP. 81, E FLAT, MAJOR.

Composed, 1809. *Dedicated to the Arch-Duke Rudolph.*

The first and only Sonata by Beethoven which has a definite programme to indicate its contents. This consists of three words : " Les adieux, l'absence, et le retour "—farewell, absence, and return. Thus the Sonata has become one of the most understandable among the later works of the master. The first movement, *adagio*, ¾ time, then *allegro*, ¼ time, E flat major, begins with the word of parting, " lebewohl," (farewell) enunciated by the three first crotchets, and painful feelings pass through the loving heart ; at first it is an anxious presentiment of parting (Marx), but with the entrance of the *allegro* comes the anguish of the actual parting, though it is not a hopeless pain,

F

nor a trouble unaccompanied by a certain happy sense of exaltation. It seems to me that in this *allegro* there are, so to speak, three moods and three phases of feeling which, in consequence of the approaching separation from a beloved object, involuntarily appear : in wonderful unison the painful sense, that after all there must be a parting ; the excited, ardent feeling of parting from an object worthy of this pain ; and the comforting assurance that the separation is not final. The motive at the beginning of the movement seems to me to correspond to the first, the octave motive which soon follows to the second, and the later motive, marked *expressivo*, to the third phase of feeling, while again the descending motive, at the conclusion of the first part, strikingly expresses quiet submission to the inevitableness of the parting. At the beginning of the second part the first state of feeling has the upper hand for some time, in a varied and characteristic form ; then the other two re-appear ; at last, however, everything is concentrated in the most impressive manner into the simple earnest tone of the farewell ; and there follows, towards the end of the movement, the warmest and most painfully-sweet embrace of the beloved object—and the parting moment arrives. The ultra fanatical upholders of the abstract laws of harmony and of material numbers, such as Fétis and Ulibischeff, are of course shocked that Beethoven should have suffered the chords, E flat and G, B flat and F, to be heard together, but in this case the higher law of ideality prevails. " Beethoven," says Marx, briefly and strikingly, " was not dealing with chords, but depicting a fond farewell, and as was ever the case with him the ideal over-ruled the material." Beethoven and the mere musician do not always go the same way. " Notes or chords are as little the essence of music as words are of poetry ; the genius of the poet forms and fashions both to his own ends." *(Marx)*. In a word, sound and harmony are here made subservient to the ideal representation. The second movement, *andante expressivo*, C minor, $\frac{3}{4}$ time, pictures the feelings of the friend who is left in lone- liness. Marx says, very justly, that the whole cha- racter of the movement shows itself in the first bars in the dragging march of the bass, and in the alternate movement of adhesion and repulsion which characterises the treble. But this feeling of desolation is accompanied by an ardent longing for the return of the absent one ; what else does that earnest melody say to us, which appears first in D, then in C major ? And now the return— the meeting—these are pourtrayed in the third movement, *vivacissime* E flat major, $\frac{6}{8}$ time. The friend is coming—go to meet him—so say the first notes, and so says the stormy rush of the semi- quavers. At the entrance of the chief motive all the pulses of life beat more quickly, and the meeting is celebrated right jubilantly. The overflowing delight now yields to a quiet contained ecstacy (the motive in

crochets) which, however, at the entrance of the G
flat major, immediately changes into sweet smiles,
of the highest delight, into caressing kisses of
supremest joy.   All these expressions of joy return
alternately, but in every fresh musical dress there
is an incessant repetition of the jubilant song of
meeting.   Then when these feelings have had full
and free vent, the tone suddenly becomes more
collected, *(poco andante)* devout and touchingly
earnest; for, as Marx well says, it would be
impossible that emotion should not mingle with
the joy of the happy ones.   They embrace once
more, but with what different feelings from when
they parted, for now both feel secure in the assurance
of everlasting union.   In this harmonious spirit the
work closes, and this spirit rests with the hearer
afterwards.   The theory of the " two principles "
mentioned in reference to op. 14 is applicable in
a very different manner to this Sonata.   In the
first and third movements there are really two
distinct spiritual forms, there is an actual dialogue.
To find out who these figures really are is quite
superfluous, and would not enhance the ideal meaning of the work.   Enough, if we know that as a
matter of course Beethoven is one person ; whether
the other form be that of a friend or lady-love is
immaterial.   Especially to be mentioned is the
masterly power with which the different feelings
in this Sonata are bound together into a firm ideal
unity, so that as a psychological necessity they
develope one out of another.

OP. 90, E MINOR.

Composed, 1814. Dedicated to Count Maurice Lichnowsky.

As clearly and definitely as the idea of the work appeared in the Sonata just mentioned, equally difficult is it to indicate it even with the least certainty in the E minor Sonata. Marx also felt this when he said that it was one of those pictures which seem to look at us with speaking, questioning glances ; they are going to speak out quite clearly and—words fail them ; as if our art had periods when it is, as it were, suspended between existence in mere tone, and in the conscious word, when one expects every moment to hear the solving word, but it is always denied. The Sonata is dedicated to Count Lichnowsky. The latter is said to have asked Beethoven what the idea of the work was, and he replied, amid roars of laughter, that he had intended to set to music the love story between the Count and his wife—a public dancer—and that he should write over the first movement, ' struggle between head and heart ; ' and over the second, ' conversation with the beloved one.' Marx was certainly right in explaining this answer of Beethoven as a joke, for it gives no clue to the meaning of the composition. Though the intention of this Sonata cannot be so clearly expressed in words as it can in other works, yet the tone-language is not without a peculiar decided character. We subscribe entirely to what Marx says of the first movement, E minor, ⅜ time—(Beethoven has written over it " with life, and with feeling and expression throughout," instead of putting any fixed *tempo* mark)—that it reveals a noble mind and energetic character, and shows what eloquence can do to combat painful doubts and fears. " A restless aspiration — that is always encountering obstacles, but is never quite exhausted, though it often timidly retreats in despair, this alternation of resolve and renunciation, of pressing forward and drawing back—is the character of the whole movement." *(Marx.)* The aim is not attained, and the soul has a foreboding of this while it struggles ; the expression, therefore, often rises to piercing sharpness and painful bitterness, but at the end the trouble seems to disappear in quiet submission to the inevitable.) The formal musical construction of the movement is masterly, a production of the utmost artistic ripeness, exquisitely finished even to the smallest details. The second movement, E major, ⅜ time, with the direction " to be played very singingly and not too fast," now flows on quietly and restfully in its rondo-song-like-form. It opens with a rich singing theme, full of earnestness, which, in the style of the rondo, constantly returns after short interruptions, between which move the most varied and joyful images, playing, as it were, around that chief form, till at last the whole softly and tenderly dies away. The movement gives the impression of a heart-idyll. As Marx says, it certainly has no new heights or aspects. But in the limited sphere which in comparison to the first this movement affords, the mind feels a sense of happiness and of contentment which restore its peace. Such seems to me the meaning of this movement with which the Sonata closes; but the feelings which it pourtrays are far removed from that comfortableness which we found before. Yet who would question their justifiableness? Do they not follow as a sort of psychological necessity from the character of the first movement? At any rate the law of raising the sentiment to a climax, in the sense which we usually take it, is not carried out in this Sonata. But this is not an absolute authoritative law for all occasions; it has, like every other law, exceptions founded on the character of the peculiar work, and the Sonata before us is surely such an exception.

OP. 101, A MAJOR.

Composed, 1813. Dedicated to the Baroness Erdmann.

This Sonata, also, belongs to those works whose meaning is, more or less, lost in words, and can only be given by hints. Marx says, " The innermost and most secret stirrings of a tender soul, to whom the desire alone is granted, not its realization, only the flights of fancy, not actual aims, not strong pithy deeds—how difficult it is to catch what it says, and to bring it to a light that shall not offend it." The first movement, *allegretto ma non troppo,*

("rather lively and with the warmest feeling," as
Beethoven has marked it) A major, $\frac{6}{8}$ time, bears the
character of fervent yearning, now timid and now
bold.   Towards what is the desire directed?   Who
can explain it?   A feeling of mystery runs through
these strains, and they are, at any rate, the production of thoroughly individual states of feeling.   Marx
finds in them nervous agitation, and even breathless-
ness.   I do not agree with him, for, to my mind, the
Sonata is too ideally, if not even somewhat too fancifully conceived for such to be the case; nor is it in
accordance with this, when Marx immediately afterwards finds in the movement, "the reserve and
speechlessness of Ottilie, without the storms through
which this, the most pleasing of Goethe's creation,
passes."   The fantasia style, though of course not in
the confused, sickly manner of later composers,
predominates decidedly in the second movement,
vivace alla marcia, F minor, $\frac{2}{4}$ time.   Marx says, very
aptly, of this movement in the march form : " Actual
deeds are not represented here, but the imagination
of deeds which might happen, dreamed strokes of
bold and lofty heroism."   The movement is quite
ætherial, so light, undulating, and bright, at the
same time not without a certain *grandezza ;* we do
not, so to speak, here meet with the tangible material
side of the march measure, *that* is made subservient
to the ideal expression.   We witness rhythmical and
tonal effects of the most original kind.   With respect
to the former, Marx brings forward the startling

entrance of the long chords, and their sudden pro-
gressions; regarding the latter, we need only to be
reminded of the frequent simultaneous sounding of
the highest and lowest, without the interposition
of the middle register. The tributary movement,
in B flat, after the manner of a trio, with its quiet
wave-like tone-lines, forms a beautiful rhythmical
contrast to the march. Following, as a third movement, is a short *adagio ma non troppo* (" slowly
and yearningly "), A minor, ⁴ tim⌐ A dull sorrow, a
gentle complaining, and then ag⌐ ⌐ ⌐ painful yearning breath through these strains. \\ ⌐ satisfies this
longing ? And how can it be sa ⌐ied ? The feelings which we experienced in the first part take
possession of the soul again. And no⌐, ⌐⌐old,
a new active life arises as it were by magic. What
is this ? It is the most confident self-consciousness,
and the happiest resolution. In this spirit the fourth
movement begins, *allegro*, (" quickly, but not too
fast, and with decision," says the master), A major,
⁴ time. The character of the gladdest resolution
could not be more strikingly represented than by the
first subject with its distinctive rhythm. This
theme enters in harmony, indeed, in double coun-
terpoint, and brings with it a brighter, brisker feeling.
After an earnest, expressive motive *(dolce)* the second
subject is heard, which strikes a child-like, cheerful
chord of nature. And when the fugue movement,
in A minor, begins, a humorous feeling makes
itself felt. As regards the formal musical construc-

tion, we find, with an exact imitation of the melody, every possible inversion and the most surprising combinations. At length on the *point d'orgue*, in the dominant E, there is a return to the first subject, and the same succession of gladdest resolution, child-like, naïve, joy, and humour, is heard again. The latter struggles out alone at last, and asserts itself triumphantly. Marx says of the whole movement: " a rich, refreshing stream of life gaily, courageously, and impetuously gushes forth." This Sonata is, as we soon discover, a very uniformly-sustained work. As regards the formal construction, it is—as was pointed out in the second movement, and can be said more or less of the whole work—the peculiar cast of the rhythm which rivets attention.

OP. 106, B FLAT MAJOR.

Composed, 1818. *Dedicated to the Arch-Duke Rudolph.*

The grandest Sonata ever composed, of colossal dimensions, a real giant, quite symphonically conceived and framed throughout. The first movement, *allegro*, B flat major, ⁴⁄₄ time, is really constructed on two chief themes; the first displaying manly boldness, power, pride, decision, and judgment; the second, womanly gentleness, grace, tenderness, softness, and devotion. The first subject opens the movement with a full chord in marked rhythm, its instant repetition a third higher, showing the ruling character only the more forcibly. Another

subject, breathing the purest mildness, is now heard;
it also is repeated an octave higher, and thus becomes
the more effective. The noble feeling of manly power
now breaks forth in full chords, the play of sounds
seems carried on with true *grandezza*, a majestic
descent of octaves from the high C follows, and
a coruscation of humour flashes from the broken
sounds of the F major chord, on which the figure of
the first theme again finds a firm footing. The
striking modulation into D brings about the transition to the second subject in G major, which now
displays itself in the most charming changes, and
assumes the most winning forms. But see, it yields
at last to an aspiring tone-figure (entrance of the C
major), out of which again there struggles an earnest
yearning song (the motive *cantabile dolce ed expressivo*),
but only to yield immediately to the strong hurrying movement of the spirit called forth by the
first theme, and with which the first part concludes.
With the second part, a new scene of a very tensive
character presents itself, rhapsodical figures produce
a highly expectant feeling, the key changes to E
flat major, the trumpet-call sounds once and again.
What does it proclaim? The first theme which
appears in the quiet depth, and gradually rises
higher and higher to a wonderful climax, which is at
last reached in the bright D major; then those
strains of deep mournful yearning are heard again,
but the first theme returns, and, at the beginning of
the third part, marches boldly forth again, fully

equipped, but accompanied with still richer orna-
ment. The process of configuration and tenor of
feeling of the first part are now repeated in a
new, peculiar, and essentially elevated style. Bold
beyond measure is the modulation into C flat after
the strong surging to and fro in broken octaves, and,
after the last outbreathings of that spirit of yearning,
the feeling gathers itself, as it were, into a focus with
the return of the first subject, which, in a shortened
form, gradually dies away; its expression is essentially modified, so that it seems as if vigour and
mildness, power and tenderness, after separately
developing themselves in a dramatic struggle, were,
at the end, closely united and reconciled. We might
say, with the poet : " Wo starkes sich mit Mildem
paaret, da giebt es einen guten Klang." What other
first movement of a Sonata can display such wonderful proportions ?   The second movement, *scherzo*, B
flat major, ¾ time, displays a restless, unstable character, a remarkable hurrying, a peculiar hunting, fleeing,
and crowding; in the chief movement especially,
an unsatisfied longing, but in the so-called *trio*, B
flat minor, in the following *presto*, and at the conclusion,
a picture of bold fantastic *bizarre* humour is unfolded,
reminding us of the wonderful, strange colouring in
the B flat minor movement. Lenz's remark, that this
movement recalls Goethe's words in " Faust :"

> " Was weben die dort um den Rabenstein ?
> Schweben auf, schweben ab, neigen sich, beugen sich.
> Vorbei ! Vorbei !"

seems to me very pertinent. The formal construction
is pre-eminently interesting in parts, inasmuch as we
meet, in the principal movement, with a rhythm
of seven bars twice over, then four bars twice, and
so seven and eight alternately. This serves only to
heighten the originality. The third movement, *adagio
sostenuto (appassionato e con molto sentimento)*, F sharp
minor, $\frac{2}{8}$ time, is a painful, ardent, yearning prayer
for light and joy, out of deep sorrow and darkness;
a tone-poem pervaded by real religious inspiration
and devotion. What could be more forcible than the
upward impulse in the first subject, issuing from the
innermost heart! At the entrance of the G major,
the first joyful beam of heavenly light penetrates the
night, but all is immediately dark again. Gleams of
joy breaks through in F sharp major, and now, when
the low D is heard, then the low F, and when the
progression is repeated higher up, what comforting,
hopeful rest breathes in these sounds! We might
here again say, with the poet, "was des Mannes
Brust ernst und tief beweget;" let that be expressed.
Fresh darkness follows, which the exalted forms
of light vainly endeavour to pierce; for a time the
gloomy night of feeling gains the fatal mastery.
But those deep unfathomable tones in F sharp major
are heard again, and produce a sense of the utmost
bliss, which is heightened by a magical modulation
from E flat to F sharp. With the change into
G major, that well of comfort is drawn from for
the last time, the primary feeling then returns. The

inward mourning becomes gradually silent, but the darkness and horror of the night are not to be chased away by the penetrating beams of the morning sun ; it is only the glimmer of the stars which falls from heaven, yet it pours a wonderful, sweet peace into the soul. Clear and simple as are the lofty ideal con-tents of this the most gigantic *adagio* of pianoforte music, equally clear and simple is its formal con-struction. At the first glance this might appear otherwise ; but closer consideration makes visible the lightest architectural grouping. Certainly every-thing is broadly and massively planned, like the first movement, for the giant's limbs have other proportions than those of ordinary men; although huge they are proportionate, and possess real beauty, symmetry, and harmony. So it is with this move-ment, the simple form of which is : *A*, chief subject, F sharp minor—Trio, D major—Fantasia ; *B*, chief subject with variations, F sharp minor, D major— Trio F sharp minor—Coda F sharp minor. We have here a peculiar union of the Sonata and rondo form. Before we part from the movement, it may be mentioned, as worthy of note, that, according to Ries, the two notes of the first bar were written by Beethoven afterwards. The two low bass notes came in apparently in the course of the move-ment, with the closer management of the chief theme, which begins strictly in the second bar; their great importance became evident to the master, and he thus recognised and supplied the

want at the beginning of the movement. Lenz
says, they seem like two steps towards the grave's
gate, calls the movement, generally, an unmeasured
wail over the ruin of all happiness. The fourth
movement is opened by an introduction, *largo*, B
flat major, ¢ time, in a free rhythmical harmonious
form. As an expressive speech, in the style of a
recitative, this highly poetic, almost dramatic prelude, is powerfully effective, stirring, as Marx says,
all the regions of the tone-world. But who can
explain this tone-mystery any further? Enough if
we feel the grandeur of the master's indignation,
if we recognize that we have not before us a mere
play of sounds, but that a deeper meaning runs
through it all. These words apply also to that
which follows the *largo*, the great three-part fugue,
allegro resoluto, B flat major, ¾ time, in which Marx
perceives the expression of a most deeply agitated
spirit, restlessly swaying up and down, coloured,
softened, and restrained by certain elegiac tones.
An image of the most restless life is displayed
before us, so gloomy often that one fancies it is
a storm with fiery lightnings and rolling thunder,
conjured up by unknown forces, an unchaining of
the dark powers. Isolated gleams of light shine
through, now and then, and a humorous impulse
is often distinctly heard. Certain it is that very
individual states of the master's mind rest in the
back-ground, and are very hard to explain; as,
indeed, in respect to form, this fugue is one of

the most difficult exercises of musical art, for the form, modulation, and working out of the themes are so peculiar that the whole cannot be followed without trouble; properly speaking, it is rather a strange union of the fugue and rondo forms than a pure, strict fugue; but the movement does not, on this account, stand any-the-less on an equality with Bach's creations, for contrapuntal art and freedom; only with this difference, that the spirit of the nineteenth century here pervades the form.* In conclusion, a word from Marx on the whole work: "Both in external proportions and in depth of meaning, the tone-poem reaches far beyond the boundaries which even Beethoven himself had hitherto reached in pianoforte music." The uniform bond which unites the four movements of the Sonata is, in my opinion, the ideal grandeur of the idea and execution; the work bears throughout the stamp of uncommonness and boldness. It might be difficult to prove that the different movements follow each other as a psychological necessity.

OP. 109, E MAJOR.

Composed, about 1821. Dedicated to Miss Brentano.

The first movement of this Sonata, in which a *vivace ma non troppo*, E major, ⁸⁄₈ time, alternates

---

* Lenz calls the Fugue: "cauchemar" and "rudis indigestaque moles ! !"

with an *adagio expressivo*, ¾ time, begins very simply,
but very significantly. The freest and most natural
harmony plays around these fleeting, hovering strains,
and the soul appears to lose itself in a fairy dream
world. Sometimes the waves seem to rise higher,
but they always grow calm again, and the stream of
sounds glides on gently and softly. Grave tones are
heard in the *adagio;* "a sharp pain," says Marx, "like
a stab at the heart," suddenly darts across the gentle
nature, and is followed by a strong, deep, ebullition
of feeling ; this solemn gloominess appears twice,
but the lovely images of the dream always regain
the mastery, and only hover around the soul the
more deliciously. Who can say what are the especial
conditions of the mind which lie at the foundation of
this ? There is something fanciful about the whole
plan and construction of this movement; despite its
depth of feeling, the movement makes the impression
of a free fantasia rather than a strict movement
of a Sonata. Marx points out, as specially significant,
the Chorale-like succession of chords towards the end.
Even Lenz cannot understand this movement ; he
calls it inconceivably weak and washy. The following second movement, *prestissimo*, E minor, ⅜ time,
bears the character of extreme dissatisfaction, of
miserable restless pressing, of an almost gloomy
chasing, involuntarily reminding us of the furies
hunting Orestes ; indeed, now and then we think of
Faust's words in his blindness : " Was schwebet
schattenhaft heran ? " This latter allusion applies

only to the motive in hollow octaves, which is heard at bar 25, and to the gleams of light, which first appear at 51 and following bars, and then flit here and there like an *ignis fatuus*. Marx finds in the movement the foreboding and the agony of death. The chord struck is an almost nervous one, highly agitated, and sensitive, but yet not sickly. As regards the formal construction, many will be reminded of the later Mendelssohnian manner; just as the march in the A major Sonata, Op. 101, recalls in some portions of the second part, Berlioz and Wagner. The construction, as well as the character of the movement, are fantasia-like throughout. The third movement, *andante molto cantabile ed expressivo*, E major, ⅜, ⅙ and ¼ time, is a theme with variations. The air comes in quietly, but firmly, decidedly, and at the same time very simply; it is a song of deep feeling, an emanation of sincere, true, restfulness of soul, a happy submission to destiny; such is the feeling it evokes. Marx calls the theme "one of those melodies full of holy devotion, in which the soul, buried quietly and deeply in itself, reflects on the past; does not think, but with the images of the past reflected in a crystal clear stream, looks back again with many an afterthought, and many a half-lost sigh, and," Marx continues, "thus far Beethoven the poet, Beethoven the musician, has written the variations; they are very fine." On a closer and deeper consideration of these variations, and a comparison of them with others, for example with Op. 57, it is, as Lenz considers, undeniable, and I myself also incline to this view, that the ideal contents of the theme do not appear as the sole spring and centre of the variations ; its character seems more or less effaced ; accordingly, this work must be judged from the point of view of formal musical construction. The variations, however, are of themselves among the most charming which Beethoven has written ; in the last variations, especially, enchanting strains are heard, sparks of humour flash forth. The first form of the theme at length harmoniously closes the whole.

OP. 110, A FLAT MAJOR.

Composed 1821.

The opening of the first movement *moderato cantabile molto expressivo*, A flat major, ¾ time, can only be called " freundlich-hold " (amiably lovely) ; it has a distant assonance with the motive of the canon in the second *finale* of Mozart's " Cosi fan tutti." After a close, a song of deep, even ardent yearning commences ; then it is suddenly heard in broken, harp-like chords, and the most laughing images flit around the soul. Happy forms pass before the mind in gay multiplicity, that song of yearning is again heard, and the first motive, which in the so-called fantasia part, is so conspicuous. The picture is richly coloured and the sense of weariness is very finely depicted in bars 6 and 13 before the end, to which the intermediate harp lispings afford a contrast. Marx finds in the movement the parting from a beloved instrument in an Ossian-like sense. Who would dispute that a touch of deep sadness pervades these tones ? There follows, as a second movement, *allegro molto*, F minor, ¾ time, which is a *scherzo* both in form and character. We meet again, although in another form, the same wild hurrying, and unquiet hunting and crowding, as in the *scherzi* of former Sonatas. Marx points out as significant the resemblance in bar 8 of the second clause to a wild popular song, " Ich bin lüderlich, du bist lüderlich," and asks, " Did there then ever come over the pure singer a dissatisfaction with the life that he was leading, a scorn of the foolish play which they call life ? " How fine, in contrast to this wild, almost intoxicating movement is the middle movement in D flat major, the so-called trio ! How fantastic and aerial, how interwoven with humorous streaks of light ! And how expressive is the Coda with those full powerful chords, broken by pauses which only make them the more impressive, and the final dying-away in soft major chords. The third movement is introduced by an *adagio ma non troppo*, B minor, ¾ time, very solemn and grave, interwoven with a recitative full of unspeakable inward trouble, which at last finds vent in a tender *arioso*, E flat minor, $\frac{12}{16}$ time. In this plaintive song, the soul fully but gently pours out all its sorrow. But we leave this repose for a scene of agitation in the fourth movement, *fuga allegro ma non troppo*, A flat major, $\frac{6}{8}$ time. The agitation flags and disappears with the re-entrance of the *arioso*, which at first expresses a yet deeper mourning and breathes more profound sighs, but, after a masterly transition, the stirring figures of the fugue again, " weben hin weben her, fluthen hin fluthen her," with ever-increasing energy to the end, where the sweeping strains of the harp are again heard, a clever imitation, an expressive souvenir of the spirit of the first movement, but, at the same time, a finely rounded and harmonious conclusion of the whole. Very individual states of feeling lie indisputably at the basis of this Sonata. Beethoven's tone-language becomes more and more peculiar, if not dark, and sometimes mysterious; the explanation in words, which can only be but a hint of the meaning, increases in difficulty, and a certain reserve in reference to these mysteries is necessary, if we would not lose ourselves in absolute phantasma. Instrumental music often offers riddles, which perhaps will never be fully solved, as the next and last of Beethoven's Sonatas gives occasion to observe.

OP. 111, C. MINOR.

Composed, 1822. Dedicated to the Arch-Duke Rudolph.

The first movement commences with a *maestoso* in C minor, $\frac{4}{4}$ time. What Titanic power! It is a volcanic eruption, powerful, solemn, dignified, full of the most striking musical expression, yet how much more full of meaning than the introduction to the "Sonata Pathétique!" The skips of a seventh in the first bars show, in a masterly manner, the deep laceration of the heart; the modulations beginning in the sixth bar have a wonderfully relieving, soothing effect; marvellously original and drastic is the change to the *allegro con brio ed appassionato*, C minor, ₄ time, which is like the distant roll of the thunder coming nearer and nearer, or the howling of the wind. The chief theme then bursts forth—an image of passionate agitation, bold defiance and the deepest gloom. With wild impetuosity the storm pursues its resistless course, the momentary abatement in the passages marked *poco ritenuto* only producing a yet more violent outburst. With the appearance of the A flat major wild flashes of humour dart in, and the spirit soars into spheres of freedom and light, but only for an instant to brace itself anew for a sterner struggle. Terrible is the fury of the storm in the second part, yet out of the night humour again struggles forth, and the soul once more soars, happily, upwards, in the clear C major. A last foaming of the dark billows, then a gradual subsidence of the dashing waves, and "tiefe Stille herrscht im Wasser, ohne Regung ruht das Meer." Equal to the grandeur of the matter of this movement is the simplicity of its formal construction, which is that of the pure, simple two-part, Sonata-form; it affords striking testimony that the greatest ends are attainable with the smallest means. The second and last movement opens with an *arietta adagio molto semplice cantabile*, C major, $\frac{9}{16}$ time, a song-like theme (Marx says, popular song) followed by four variations which resolve themselves into a sort of fantasia, to which is coupled a new variation of the air, connected with which is a tributary movement, which, uniting with the first eight bars of the theme, shakes and bass figures, thus brings in a Coda and conclusion. Such, in bare words, is the simple formal process, the skeleton, so to speak, of the movement, but what about the contents? Kullak says that the Sonata sinks into insipidity in the variations. Lenz thinks that strange and marvellous ideas had been conceived, but that the *arietta*, that divine exhalation, loses itself in running figure work; finally, Marx says, the *arietta* with the strangely dissevered melodies, with the deep descending bass, with the change into A minor, with the emphasized notes E... E... sounding throughout, recalls those elegiac melodies, the funeral songs. Marx then continues: "Variations carry out the suggestions of the arietta; who can say all, and who can explain all?" "I have hidden much therein," Goethe once said, in a similar case. Elsewhere Marx speaks of the composition as a deep-feeling theme, overflowing with tender, profound melancholy, carried out with the greatest steadiness, but with ever increasing richness, now subdued, now pleasantly stirred, but

returning to the elegiac primary tone of feeling
rousing up with new courage, and afterwards sinking
into the deepest despondency. It is quite inconceivable to me how Kullak can feel any insipidity in
these strains, and for the same reason also I can
but pity Lenz's regret, for both seem to me only
to have grasped the shell, without penetrating to
the kernel. On the other hand, one can agree with
Marx that Beethoven has " hidden much " in this
movement,   I cannot describe the impression which
it always makes upon me. It seems as if we had
an echo from the loftiest ideal and spiritual regions,
the language, which is simply untranslatable into
words, of the soul soaring to the heavenly regions
with fervent and holy rapture. When I thus com-
pletely lose myself in this tone-world, the last
scene of the second part of Goethe's " Faust "—
Faust's transfiguration—always occurs to me. We
may find in the second strophe of the *arietta*,
" Zeugen menschlicher Bedürftigkeit," " Spuren von
schroffen Erdenwegen," but only " dass ja das
Nichtige Alles verflüchtige ; " such is the tendency
of this tone-creation. How wonderfully does the
deep, fervent song of the arietta ever strive after
the heavenly, after lighter spheres, just as Faust
was ever lifted higher—" steigt hinan zu höherem
Kreise."   In fancy one sees the hovering forms
of the *pater profundus, pater seraphicus,* and *pater
ecstaticus,* when, full of the fantasy of the tone-
movement, we follow it, now in the lowest, then

in the highest tone-regions. Towards the end does not a feeling take possession of us akin to that in the lines :

"Nebelnd um Felsenhöh—spür ich so eben
Regend sich in der Näh'—ein Geisterleben.
Die Wölkchen werden klar ;—ich seh' bewegter Schaar,
Seliger Knaben,—los von der Erde Druck,
Im Kreis gesellt—die sich erlaben
An neuem Lenz und Schmack—der obern Welt."

If any one says to me, "You are writing mere idle fancies," I certainly cannot produce proof to the contrary, but I only write what I truly feel. And is it, then, so incredible that there should be a point of contact between the greatest of German word-poets, and the greatest of German tone-poets? Enough if it is only granted that here, as in all deep instrumental music, there lies a mystery, a mystery which always reveals itself more or less according to the nature of the imagination that contemplates it. Without imagination no musical work can be understood, least of all a creation of Beethoven ; mere musical knowledge, mere acquaintance with the laws of composition do not suffice.* To return once more and finally to the second movement of the Sonata ; these are no ordinary variations. They were not written by Beethoven the musician, but by Beethoven the tone-

---

* Of these strains, also, we might say again, with Beethoven, "thousands do not understand them."

poet ; they are creations such as he alone could produce, such, for example, as he has given us in the
Sonata, Op. 57. Kullak says in the work from
which we have already quoted that " the variations
fail in that lofty intellectual development which
cannot endure the monotony of repetition except
as a brief relaxation from a lyrical strain; the
variations have no leading thought and no living
energy, for which reason they should have been
placed in the middle, not at the end of a great
work." Whatever truth these words may contain,
they do not apply to the variations in question.
Variations, such as Op. 111, are like an ideal
emanation of the theme, or, to use a simile, are
the pure rays radiating from the theme, enthroned
like a sun in a firmament of exalted peace. These
variations are only a deeper and more spiritual
expression of the theme. The formal side of the
variation form retreats, an ideal *denouement* is
involuntarily accomplished in free, unfettered fancy.
Do not these so-called variations form a satisfactory
conclusion ? Is a concluding movement still wanting ?
Schindler says, yes ; that he asked the master why
he did not write a third movement, corresponding to
the two first, and Beethoven replied that time failed
him for a third movement ; he was therefore obliged
to extend the second. Believe this who will. Could
Beethoven have found time to give this extension to
the second movement if it had failed him for a third ?
A nice contradiction. And even if Beethoven did give

utterance to this speech, it is well-known how laconic his answers often were, and how readily he cut short inquisitive, intrusive questioners. Perhaps he thought, too, with Mephistopheles, " Das Beste was du weisst, darfst du den Buben doch nicht sagen." I consider that a third movement was psychologically as impossible as a tenth symphony.

As Gervinus says, after a discussion of Shakespeare's latest works, so we say, " With the C minor Sonata, Beethoven finished his course as a Sonata-maker, and, like Prospero, broke and buried fathoms deep the magic wand of his tone-poetry. Happy the disciple who recovers this treasure."

No one has yet found it, notwithstanding the high attainments of Franz Schubert and others, and the Beethoven Sonata stands, in reality, unrivalled in original beauty, an inexhaustible well of the purest wonderment, a glittering crown of stars to all who seek after pure musical forms.

Fifth Part.

RETROSPECTIVE.—CONCLUDING REMARKS.

IF we now glance over the rich world which the Beethoven Sonatas reveal to us, we shall see that these works divide themselves—one might say involuntarily—into several groups. We meet with works which evidently belonged to Beethoven's early youth; with works in which, although riper, the influence of Beethoven's predecessors, Haydn and Mozart, was still very noticeable and dominant; with works in which Beethoven's independence became paramount, and the Haydn-Mozart influence banished; and finally with works in which Beethoven appeared in his complete individuality, the former foundations having entirely disappeared. The following groups may then be formed:

GROUP I.—Op. 6, 49, 79.
GROUP II.—Op. 2, 7, 10, 13, 14, 22.
GROUP III.—Op. 26, 27, 28, 31.
GROUP IV.—Op. 53, 54, 57, 78, 81, 90, 101, 106, 109, 110, 111.

But the last five works of group IV., as belonging to Beethoven's so-called Third Period, are so essentially different from the others, that they might lay claim to an independant subdivision and group. There would thus be comprised in

GROUP V.—Op. 101, 106, 109, 110, 111.

Before characterising and analysing these works, we must emphatically state that it is not our intention to set up lifeless limitations, but to seek some landmarks in this rich and vast tone-world. If we keep in mind that it is not necessary to force any work into a barren category, if we recognize that the groups are themselves united together by fine threads—for the succeeding always rests its basis on the preceding one—a certain systematic arrangement will only the more easily separate a particular work from the others, and set it in a light so much the more original.

With respect to the different groups, group 1 certainly needs no further consideration. As general characteristics of the works of the second group, besides the basis of the Haydn-Mozart style of writing, the following may be mentioned ; concerning the substance, a fixed, leading, poetical, fundamental idea is still more or less wanting, and this deficiency pervades the character of the works which have least meaning and purpose ; concerning the form, it has been prevailingly prompted by mere custom ; the relation of the keys is often the only bond between

the movements by which a similar and uniform tone
is as far as possible produced.   The so-called second
subject still occupies, as with Mozart, a great deal of
space, makes its independance felt, while in the more
perfect later works the first subject is the decisive
part of the movement, the second theme yielding to
it in importance, by which a much stricter unity is
attained.   The most important work of this group,
in many ways stretching far beyond it, and in parts
even surpassing works of the third group, is undoubtedly the D major Sonata, Op. 10.   In group
III there appear so many waverings and leanings
towards Haydn and Mozart, (for example, Op. 26,
28, 31^1, 31^3,) that single movements might still be
ranked in the second group, but the intellectual
basis is, in general, different, a definite poetical
meaning comes out more clearly, the short characteristic chief motive of the works of the following
group appears.   The most prominent work of the
third group is indisputably, the C sharp minor
Sonata, which, with the exception of the second
movement, might certainly be placed in the next
group.   The following characteristic signs appear in
the works of the fourth group:

The uniform, definite purport of the Sonata;   the
short, characteristic chief subject;   the exclusive
employment of the latter in the so-called fantasia
part; the working-up of the chief theme in the Coda,
which obtains thereby a certain independence and
exclusiveness; the limitation of the second thought

to its place in the first, and repetition in the so-called third part; the frequent abandonment of the four and even three-movement form, with the predominance of the two-movement form; and the more symphonic character of the Sonata, that is as regards the form and working out of the thought, not with respect to its origination, and to the polyphonic character of the symphony.

The most valuable work of this group is the Sonata, Op. 57, while the Sonatas, Op. 54, and Op. 78, properly belong to it only on account of their special formal construction; in their matter they are far surpassed by works of earlier groups.

Finally, concerning group V., the peculiarities of the works belonging to it are : the appearance of the polyphonic, contrapuntal element; the return to the three and four-movement form; the disappearance of the two-movement form (except in Op. 111); the resumption of the small sonatina and march form; and the highly individual subjective contents.

The fugue form is more freely and fancifully treated than with Bach; it may be called a blending of the fugue and rondo form, in which charming tributary movements enliven ever and anew the cold fugue form although we must at the same time admit that a certain amount of harshness is perceptible. The abandonment of the two-movement form in the first four works, the re-appearance of the great independent *adagio* in Op. 106; this fundamental deviation from the style of construction in the former group with its compressed, precise forms, might lead it to be supposed that these did not satisfy Beethoven's intentions, and that he had perceived a certain discrepancy. But the extension of fixed forms does not lead us to expect their total abandonment. Besides Beethoven returns to the two-movement form in Op. 111, and the different movements of the last five works, with the exception perhaps of Op. 106, show no signs of a uniform plan throughout. One must also bear in mind that usages and proprieties could not unconditionally influence the now independent Beethoven. He adhered to settled forms in so far only as they served as a means for the intended ideal expression. This was most clearly apparent in his last quartetts, in which he drew all available artistic forms into his creative circle, regardless whether he had used them before or not. In the Symphonies, with the exception of the last, Beethoven never departs from the customary form, wisely reflecting that the universality for which such works are destined only accustoms itself very slowly to anything new. The Sonata and quartett gave him better scope, for works of this kind, on account of their limited musical material, and the absence of the multiform tone-colouring of the great orchestra, require for their appreciation a deeper and more educated musical sympathy and fancy.

Marx, in his " Music of the 19th century and Beethoven," has formed another division of the Sonatas, founded on his views of the nature of music.

According to Marx music is threefold : mere tone-play, language of feeling (music of the soul), and music of the mind (ideal representation), the latter being found in the highest degree and almost exclusively with Beethoven. A great truth lies at the basis of this division, especially if, like Marx, we do not draw a hard and fast line between the sections where they vitally join each other. Music is, and remains, pre-eminently, an art of the emotional fancy ; feeling, the music of the soul, is the ideal centre; and it appears in mere tone-play—for otherwise Hanslick was right in saying that music is only a sounding arabesque. Feeling pervades also music of the mind—the ideal representation—for how else could intellect and ideal representation find any expression in sounds, if feeling were not the connecting medium ? This division can here only lay claim to full force and truth in so far as this or that feature is the leading one in any particulaa work. Marx then classifies thus :—

MERE TONE-PLAY.

Op. 2, No. 3 ; op. 10, Nos. 1 and 2 ; op. 14 ; op. 22, op. 27 op. 31, Nos. 1 and 3 ; op. 53 ; op. 54 : op. 78 ; op. 106.

EMOTIONAL LIFE.

Op. 2, Nos, 1 and 2 ; op. 7 ; op. 10, No 3 ; op. 13 ; op. 26 ; op. 28 ; op. 31, No. 2 ; op. 90.

IDEAL REPRESENTATION.

Op. 27, No. 2 ; op. 57 ; op. 81 ; op. 101 ; op. 109 ; op. 110 ; op. 111.

This grouping evinces, as indeed we need not to be told, that Marx had a deep insight into the sense and spirit of the Sonatas. In some particulars, however, many will be of another opinion ; the place given to the Sonata, Op. 106, especially, will doubtless be disputed. Marx says, at the beginning, although none of the Sonatas, in the sphere of pure tone-play, are without a deeper meaning for the soul, yet they require technical capacity, first of all, and with it that " feeling " which comes instinctively to musically gifted and skilful performers. As if Op. 57, Op. 101, &c., did not also require technical capacity, and as if in Op. 106, mere "feeling" would be any more use to us than in any other works. That Op. 106 belongs to the third group appears to me beyond doubt. I think also that in the Sonatas, Op. 10, Nos. 1 and 2, Op. 22, Op. 27, No. 1, considered as a whole, not tone-play, but music of the soul predominates; again, Op. 31, No. 2, rises to ideal representation, which Marx also suggests as " perhaps demonstrable." Op. 6, Op. 49, and Op. 79, belong to the first group as a matter of course.

A general arrangement of Beethoven's Sonatas, according to the keys and the *tempi*, is not without interest. The works, Op. 6, Op. 49, Op. 79, may be justly passed over here; on the other hand, the so-called trios, for example, when they are in different keys to the minuett and scherzo, also the important intermediary movements, like the arioso in Op. 110, may be reckoned separately. Hence the following result :—

A. Tempi.

25 movements are in $\frac{2}{4}$ time.

24   ,,   ,, $\frac{3}{4}$

26   ,,   ,, $\frac{4}{4}$

3   ,,   ,, $\frac{2}{8}$

10   ,,   ,, $\frac{6}{8}$

2   ,,   ,, $\frac{9}{8}$

1   ,,   ,, $\frac{12}{8}$

1   ,,   ,, $\frac{9}{16}$

1   ,,   ,, $\frac{12}{16}$

In addition to this $\frac{9}{16}$ and $\frac{12}{32}$ time appear in the Sonata, Op. 111, which alone has $\frac{9}{16}$ time, as Op. 57 has $\frac{12}{8}$, and Op. 110 $\frac{12}{16}$ time.

B. Keys.

11 movements are in C major.

7   ,,   ,,   C minor.

2   ,,   ,,   C sharp minor.

5   ,,   ,,   D flat major.

7   ,,   ,,   D major.

4   ,,   ,,   D minor.

12   ,,   ,,   E flat major.

2   ,,   ,,   E flat minor.

6   ,,   ,,   E major.

3   ,,   ,,   E minor.

9   ,,   ,,   F major.

7   ,,   ,,   F minor.

2   ,,   ,,   F sharp major.

1 movement is in   F sharp minor.

5 movements are in G major.

2   ,,   ,,   G minor.

9   ,,   ,,   A flat major.

1 movement is in   A flat minor.

7 movements are in B flat major.

2   ,,   ,,   B flat minor.

The favourite keys of the great masters are some-times spoken of, and C minor is mentioned as Beet-

hoven's favourite key. The Sonatas do not confirm
this ; for in them C major, E flat major, F major, A
flat major, stand foremost. The idea that every
key has something characteristic and is specially
adopted only for the expression of certain states
of mind and feeling, has been widely opposed, among
others, by the most important connoisseurs of music ;
for example, by Hauptmann ("Natur der Harmonik
und Metrik.")   But in every key there exist the
same relations between intervals, and the pitch
gradually becomes higher with time; C major, the
fundamental key, is higher now than it was a
hundred years ago; consequently this theory is
only a self-deception, and the transposition of a
piece of music into another key cannot alter the
character of it.   According to Schindler, Beethoven
maintained the characteristic character of the different keys.   Schindler says (Biography ii., 156,
3rd edition) : "The opinions put forth by Beethoven
were based on a thorough knowledge of every key ;
the pitch may move a whole tone higher or lower
than the ear is accustomed to hear, but transposition
is quite out of the question, because the central
point in the musical system must be in an immove-
able position ; the pitch of the orchestra has imper-
ceptibly become higher ; in like manner, also, our
feeling for the 'psyche' of the keys, which requires
that every key should have its place in the scale,
which indeed the ancients duly recognized ; but
transposition is a sudden variation of at least half

a tone, by which the feeling is suddenly removed into another sphere, because the ‘psyche’ is violently forced out of the first combination of sounds into another; if, therefore, there were no difficulty in distinguishing C sharp major from the enharmonic D flat major, the ear would be directed into a second line; there would be the sense of the subtle difference between hard and soft, and then the characteristic signs of both these keys.” So far Beethoven briefly and to the point. It may be then most confidently stated that he was not governed by mere caprice in the choice of keys, but by the idea of the work and the nature of the particular movement. Can one imagine such characteristic works as the C sharp minor Sonata, the F minor Sonata, Op. 57, the C minor Sonata, Op. 111, in other keys? Would not the pictures of character which these works unfold to us become quite obliterated, and colourless? But I only wish to throw out a suggestion with regard to other points of view in which the Sonatas may still be considered.

A comparison of Beethoven’s Sonatas with his quartetts and symphonies will lead the impartial observer to this among other conclusions, that as regards the working out of the several works, the union and arrangement of the different movements, Beethoven, if we may use the expression, sometimes took things more easily than in his quartetts and symphonies. Kullak says that Beethoven’s weakness lies in the inequality of the style of a great number of his works. This is evidently saying too much, and does not touch the later Beethoven. But it may apply indeed to the Haydn-Mozart period of the master, when, as was shown in the discussion of the different Sonatas in the former part, Beethoven now and then loses his cue. The heel of Achilles, in a great number of the Beethoven Sonatas, is to be found in the minuetts, which certainly might just as well have been omitted, without intenfering with the general configuration of the Sonata, and which seem to exist only because the four-movement form happened to be in vogue then. This is also directly confirmed by Beethoven himself. To wit, Schindler relates (Part II, page 215) that on the occasion of a proposed collective edition of the Sonatas, in which the poetical idea lying at the foundation of them was to be stated, Beethoven considered whether it would not tend to the attainment of greater unity, if some of the four-movement Sonatas, written at an earlier period when the four-movement form was the only one in accepted usage, were to be changed into the three-movement form. The Sonatas, Op. 2, Nos. 2 and 3, Op. 22, Op. 26, Op. 28, Op. 31, No. 3, and according to our ideas, Op. 27, No. 2, could certainly dispense with their minuetts without disadvantage. To this we may also add that, as it seems to me, in a great number of the minuetts or *scherzi*, the middle movement, the so-called trio, or minor, is, in a remarkable manner, the most original or at

least the most characteristic part of the movement.
I refer only to Op. 2, No. 3, Op. 7, Op. 10, No. 3,
O. 22, Op. 26, Op. 27, Op. 31, No. 3.

The study of Beethoven's Sonatas is no easy one,
whether we consider the intellectual or the technical
part. As he took his starting point from Haydn and
Mozart, it seems urgently required that we should not
begin with him, but with his predecessors, for with
Beethoven we come to the final point, " the entrance
into the ideal " *(Marx)* Marx has provided a capital
help in his " Appendix " to the Biography of Beethoven, and also in his work, " Guide to the Perform-
ance of Beethoven's Pianoforte Music." Both cannot
be too warmly recommended to the lovers of Beethoven, although I must content myself with thus
referring to them. But it must be especially
mentioned that as regards the technique, Marx
gives the following gradation : Op. 6, Op. 49, Op.
79, Op. 14, Op. 13, Op. 2, Op. 10, Op. 22, Op.
26, Op. 28, Op. 7, Op. 54, Op. 31, Op. 90, Op. 27,
Op. 81, Op. 101, Op. 110, Op. 57, Op. 109, Op. 53,
Op. 111, Op. 106, while, with respect to the intellectual comprehension, the progress from the
understandable to the profound, he gives this order :
Op. 2, Op. 13, Op. 14, Op. 22, Op. 54, Op. 53, Op.
78, (Op. 26, Op. 10, Cp. 7, Op. 28, Op. 31, Op. 27,
Op. 57), Op. 81, Op. 90, Op. 106, Op. 101, Op. 110,
Op. 109, Op. 111, in which certainly no regard was
taken to the very diversified point of view taken in
Op. 2, Op. 14, Op. 10, Op. 31, Op. 27. Without

deep inward life, and spontaneous fancy, no great musical work can be comprehended, not to speak of a Beethoven creation.

Beethoven's Sonatas have appeared in various editions. Among the best and cheapest is Hallberger's, of Stutgart, the edition being uniform with that of Haydn and Mozart's Sonatas. Louis Köhler, of Königsberg, has recently undertaken a duet arrangement of the Beethoven Sonatas. They are beautifully got up and published at a very moderate price by Henry Litolff (Brunswick). The edition includes also the Sonatas for the pianoforte, with accompaniments for the violin, 'cello, &c. Köhler has well confuted any objections we might raise against the four-hand arrangement, and we cannot but agree with the reasons which he gives in justification of his undertaking: that this duet-edition is especially adapted to the requirements of less technically accomplished players, for only by these means can the approach to the profoundest Sonatas be facilitated, since these also offer the greatest technical difficulties.

Thus will the Beethoven music extend into an ever-widening circle, the number of Beethoven's friends will increase from year to year, and the temple of true musical beauty will be more widely opened and become a greater blessing to mankind.

FINIS.

G. HILL, STEAM PRINTER, WESTMINSTER BRIDGE ROAD.

www.ingramcontent.com/pod-product-compliance
Lightning Source LLC
Chambersburg PA
CBHW020759020726
47495CB00008B/2512